Spelling by Hand

Teaching Spelling
in a Waldorf School

to my teachers

Michael and Craig

thank you

Spelling by Hand

Teaching Spelling in a Waldorf School

A Guide for Class Teachers

by

Jeremy Herrmann

Waldorf
PUBLICATIONS
RESEARCH INSTITUTE FOR *Waldorf* EDUCATION

Printed with support from the Waldorf Curriculum Fund

Published by:

Waldorf Publications at the
Research Institute for Waldorf Education
38 Main Street
Chatham, NY 12037

Title: *Spelling by Hand*
 Teaching Spelling in a Waldorf School:
 A Guide for Class Teachers
Author: Jeremy Herrmann
Layout: Ann Erwin
Proofreading: Melissa Merkling

Table of Contents

Introduction: Why Teach Spelling?

Through all of our lessons in a Waldorf school, we aim to foster children's healthy relationship to authority, to meet their inner developmental needs, and to develop their capacities for willing, feeling, and thinking. The answer to the question, "Why teach spelling?" is supported by these key principles of Waldorf education.

As the basis for each spelling lesson, the teacher fosters the children's healthy relationship to authority through bringing consciousness to how grown-ups spell words. Throughout the grades, the children's inner needs for security, social relationship, and conceptual thinking are met through the types of spelling words they learn. The focus on careful listening and careful looking required by the children when spelling will develop within them a more refined capacity for observing and listening to their world.

For answers to the questions "What do we teach of spelling?" and "How do we teach it?" I hope that this book will serve you well. In offering what to teach, I have attempted to be economical and thoughtful because I acknowledge there are many and varied important parts of the school day that exist beyond spelling instruction. In offering how to teach spelling, I have provided clear recommendations based on my research, and I leave open the possibility for these ideas to serve as your springboard for creative teaching. It is with great pride, joy, and excitement that I share this book with you.

Teaching Spelling in a Waldorf School

Rudolf Steiner provided several indications regarding the teaching of spelling. An effective teacher of spelling incorporates these indications with contemporary spelling education research, the developmental needs of the children, and practical considerations. Additionally, he or she understands the teaching of spelling within the context of other reading, language arts and life lessons.

Once these understandings are reached, the recommended learning objectives and classroom activities outlined in this book can provide Waldorf schools with a fun, economical, and thoughtful spelling curriculum as a foundation from which teachers are free to teach effectively.

Rudolf Steiner on Spelling

Here is a summary of Rudolf Steiner's ideas on spelling. When the correct spellings of words are taught to children, it should not be introduced as truth in the same way that $4 = 2 + 2$ is true, but rather should be introduced based on a respect for the living authority of grown-ups. Instead of a teacher saying to a child, "This is how this word is spelled," the teacher may say something like, "This is how grown-ups spell this word." Children come to school in order to learn how to enter into the world of grown-ups. Underlying all lessons on spelling should be a respect for the living authority of grown-ups.

Children who spell words correctly use careful listening and careful looking. When a child accurately listens to each sound in a given word and identifies the appropriate matching letters, he or she is likely to be able to spell most words correctly. However, careful listening alone will not always result in correct spelling. Some words exist which are spelled differently from how they sound. Children who use careful looking when reading such words are able to spell more challenging words correctly.

While correct spelling is important, if it is overemphasized or brought in the wrong way, the effects are not desirable. The well-being of the whole child is always more important than any one particular skill, such as spelling. We are to teach spelling in such a way that avoids fettering children with rigid rules and thus allows their souls to remain flexible and free.

Developmental Stages in Learning to Spell

Reading and spelling require visual and auditory processing in the brain. The right hemisphere of the brain used for visual processing starts developing for reading around age four and allows young children to read by guessing at a word based on the first and last letter and length of the word. Although a child of age four is technically able to learn to read using the right hemisphere of the brain, this type of guess-reading is ultimately harmful to reading and spelling development.

The left hemisphere of the brain starts developing for reading around age seven and allows children to sound out words and spell correctly by paying careful attention to each letter in a given word.

Both hemispheres of a child's brain are not fully developed for the tasks of reading and spelling until closer to age nine. If a child is taught to read and spell too early in development, the right hemisphere of the brain is overly taxed. This imbalance can show itself in the later grades as poor reading comprehension and poor spelling.

The tasks of reading and spelling are intimately connected. The processes for learning how to read and learning how to spell are the same, except that we advance through a given stage of reading development prior to advancing through the same stage of spelling development. Reading a word is easier than spelling a word. Children are able to read more words than they are able to spell. Just because a child is able to read a given word, does not necessarily mean that spelling the same word accurately will follow. If a child is able to spell a given word, then reading that word is inevitable. In a certain sense, spelling represents the highest level of mastery of language. In order for a child to learn how to spell a word, first the skills required to read the word must be in place. It is possible for an excellent or weak reader to be an excellent or weak speller.

The sequential stages which children move through when learning reading and spelling are well documented according to which types of words children at any given age are able to learn. Generally, children move through three major stages when learning spelling. Children in the early grades learn how to spell regular words (i.e., words that are spelled exactly as they sound). Next, children learn how to spell pattern words (i.e., words that apply a common spelling pattern or spelling rule). In the later grades, children learn to spell irregular words (i.e., words that are not spelled as they sound and do not follow common patterns or rules).

A Waldorf Approach to Spelling Instruction

The approach to teaching spelling in a Waldorf school described in this guide is consistent with Rudolf Steiner's indications about teaching spelling and with mainstream spelling research. This spelling program was created to be economical and thoughtful. This spelling work is also fun, particularly in the early grades, when it is most important to foster children's love of language. Spelling practice described in this guide should be used in balance with, but should not replace, the meaningful opportunities children have to explore language through listening, speaking, reading and writing.

This program is *economical* in that it concisely offers the most important information related to teaching spelling. Children already learn a great deal about spelling naturally through the meaningful experiences they have with language; however, explicit spelling instruction which focuses on teaching the most important aspects of spelling is necessary for most children to develop into proficient spellers. The program is *thoughtful* in that it matches spelling instruction to the developmental level of the individual child at each given age.

Keys to the Program

This spelling program teaches spelling as a living concept and recommends small amounts of repetitive practice each day for the best results. The spelling lessons should progress from reading to spelling, from whole-class questioning to individual questioning, and from homogeneous to heterogeneous practice.

Teach spelling as a living concept. Spelling should be taught as a living concept. Beginning in first grade, children learn the most foundational spelling concepts. As children discover and learn new spelling concepts, they build upon what they already know. Spelling instruction of this type does not merely teach children how to spell individual words. Rather, children learn how to think about spelling and thus become lifelong learners of new words.

Use small amounts of repetitive practice. In the first grade, approximately five to fifteen minutes per main lesson during language arts blocks can be dedicated to explicit spelling instruction. Most of the spelling practice activities recommended in this program require only five minutes of class time, and thus a few different activities can be accomplished each day. A teacher must be sensitive to how the children respond in order to adjust how long or short the spelling practice should last. If spelling practice lasts too long, the children become restless. If the spelling practice is too short, then all children are not able to fully engage in a meaningful way. The success of the program depends on small amounts of repetitive practice of the same activities each day toward spelling mastery.

Begin with reading skills. Effective spelling instruction should begin with teaching the skills required for reading a word and progress toward teaching of the skills required for spelling a word. For example, looking at a letter and identifying the sound it represents is a reading skill, while listening to a sound and identifying the corresponding letter is a spelling skill. Reading is an easier task than spelling. Instruction which focuses first on reading a given word will give children the foundation necessary for learning to spell.

Begin with whole-class responses. Each new spelling activity should be practiced as a whole class when it is first introduced. The whole class relies on the most competent children as the majority of the class becomes more familiar and comfortable with the responses expected. With each new day, the teacher should slightly modify the activity from whole-class response toward requiring more participation from individual children. A given activity has been mastered when a teacher is able to call on any individual child who was not raising a hand and to receive a correct response consistently.

Begin by teaching all words of the same type: homogeneous/heterogeneous practice. Once a class has mastered spelling a certain type of word, spelling those words should be practiced heterogeneously with other words that have been learned until mastered. When a class is first practicing a group of words homogeneously, they know that all of the words that they are being asked to spell follow the same structure or pattern. The ultimate goal is not for the children to learn how to spell words in isolation during spelling practice, but to be able to spell correctly while writing. In order to achieve this goal, once a group of words is learned to mastery homogeneously, those words should be mixed heterogeneously in spelling practice with other types of words that have already been learned.

Summary. The success of this Waldorf spelling program, in which spelling is taught as a living concept, depends on small amounts of repetitive practice of the same activities each day toward spelling mastery. Spelling instruction throughout the grades should progress from reading to spelling, from whole-class questioning to individual questioning, and from homogeneous to heterogeneous practice.

Regular Words – Grades 1 and 2

Explicit spelling instruction in the early grades should focus solely on careful listening and the auditory processing required for proficient spelling. With focus only on the phonetic skills and auditory processing required for correct spelling, first and second graders are given age-appropriate practice with words while they avoid the harmful effects of learning to read too early in their development. Careful listening will be the foundation for correct spelling in subsequent stages of spelling development.

Children in the early grades should learn how to spell words that are spelled exactly as they sound. Spelling instruction with this focus meets children at this stage in their development by presenting them with words in which the spellings make sense. As a result, children learn that the world is a safe and sensible place. If children are exposed to challenging spelling words too early, they may experience uncertainty and randomness.

For this reason, focusing spelling instruction on word families and sight words is not recommended in grades 1 and 2. Non-intuitive spelling conventions (e.g., the word *knight* beginning with the letter "k," the words *pie* and *my* rhyming but being spelled differently, etc.) may naturally arise for children during the language arts experiences they have involving speaking, listening, reading, and writing. However, in grades 1 and 2, such irregularities should not be explicitly focused on to improve spelling ability.

Alliteration

In the beginning of grade 1, when a letter of the alphabet is introduced, the teacher asks the children to identify as many words as they can that begin with that sound. This is not an activity for only one day of class, but should be repeated for several consecutive days using the same sound and, likely, most of the same words each day. Alliteration with a given sound can be left to rest when a class has practiced it for so many days that a teacher is able to randomly call on any child in the class and the child is easily able to say at least five words that begin with the given sound. A more challenging task that a teacher may consider is having the children identify words that all *end* with a given sound.

The words that children say when alliterating do not need to be written by the teacher on the chalkboard or by the children in their main lesson books. The spoken alliteration holds more value than the written alliteration at this stage of development. Furthermore, one does not need to carry out this alliteration activity with every letter of the alphabet. Focusing on a handful of sounds and giving each sound several days of repetitive practice is more effective than going through every sound for one or two days each.

Rhyming

Rhyming may be carried out in a similar way. A teacher comes into class prepared with a word family that contains many rhyming words. (A list of such words is provided in the Word Lists section.) The teacher asks the children to identify as many rhyming words as they can. Again, this activity should be repeated with the same word family daily for consecutive days or even weeks until every child in the class is able to independently offer at least five rhyming words in that family. The words do not need to be written down. The activity of rhyming is more important. When rhyming, a class may begin to work with hand spelling.

Hand Spelling

- Show a closed fist and say the word.

- Extend your thumb and say the onset sound of the word.

- Extend all of your remaining fingers at once and say the remaining rhyming sound of the word.

- Close your fist and repeat the whole word.

Hand spelling and finger spelling (described later) are useful in first and second grade in order to make the experience of spelling more concrete for children. Each abstract sound is connected with a physical finger, and then symbolically they are all pulled back together. Although in the second half of first grade, the class will begin to work with a new set of spelling activities, the work with rhyming and alliteration may continue through the end of second grade and beyond. Rhyming and alliteration require only a few minutes of class time if organized economically and are foundational activities for spelling development.

CVC Words

In the second half of first grade, once the class has been introduced to the alphabet, they are ready to begin to practice spelling CVC (consonant-vowel-consonant) words (e.g., *cat, top, mix*, etc.). This is the first stage of learning correct spelling. Children in this stage of spelling development are commonly challenged when trying to identify the correct short vowel sound in a given CVC word. A teacher introduces one or two of the short vowel sounds at a time with the intention of ultimately moving from homogeneous to heterogeneous practice. A class can practice discrimination of the short vowel sounds through the following two activities.

Letter Cards – The teacher has five pieces of white cardboard with a different vowel written on each one. The teacher shows a given card to a child and the child says the short vowel sound that the letter would make in a CVC word. This is repeated consecutively for each child in the class.

Spoken Sounds – All children stand in a row at their desks. The teacher says a short vowel sound. Each child in turn says the name of the letter that makes that sound and then sits down. This is repeated consecutively for each child in the class.

The *Letter Cards* activity practices a skill required for reading and the *Spoken Sounds* activity logically follows as a slightly more challenging activity that practices a skill required for spelling. As the class begins to move toward individual responses in the *Letter Cards* activity, work with whole-class response to the *Spoken Sounds* activity may begin.

Finger Spelling

When learning how to read and spell words throughout first and second grade, children may use finger spelling. Finger spelling is an extension of hand spelling used during rhyming. Hand spelling represents only the onset and

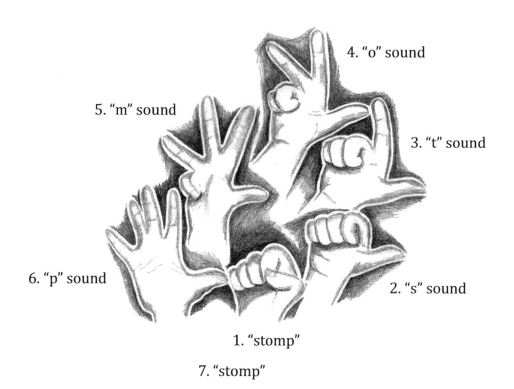

4. "o" sound

5. "m" sound

3. "t" sound

6. "p" sound

2. "s" sound

1. "stomp"

7. "stomp"

---

rhyming sounds in a word while finger spelling separately expresses each sound in a word. The guidelines for finger spelling are as follows:

- Show a closed fist and say the word.

- Extend your thumb and say the first sound or letter of the word.

- Extend your pointer finger and say the second sound or letter of the word.

- Extend your middle finger and say the third sound or letter of the word.

- Close your fist and repeat the whole word.

The following three activities using finger spelling can help to move the class from practicing reading skills to practicing spelling skills.

Reading with Finger Spelling – CVC words are written in a list on the chalkboard. The children say a given word and then, using finger spelling, separate and say the sound made by each letter, and then say the given word again.

Listening with Finger Spelling – The teacher says a word. The children finger spell the word.

Spelling Aloud with Finger Spelling – The teacher spells a word aloud. The children say and finger spell the word aloud.

These spelling practice activities are just the beginnings of the work that can be done with children to practice spelling. (A comprehensive list is provided in the Spelling Activities and Games section.) Any variations of a spelling activity that allow children to experience and to practice some spelling skill in a new way are useful. A creative teacher can be flexible in how to structure and vary each activity each day in order to economically provide the children with a variety of opportunities to play with words in many different ways.

Imagination

Whenever possible, a teacher may use age-appropriate images that appeal to a child's heart in order to explain spelling convention. For example, in order to explain the silent "e," a teacher may say something like, "The 'e' is such a good friend to the 'a' that he just quietly listens while the 'a' is allowed to be his true self" or, "When a letter makes a long vowel sound, it sings, and when it makes a short vowel sound, it whispers." The children benefit when teachers create and tell stories in order to enliven spelling instruction so long as the stories do not distract or deter from the focus of the lesson.

Writing in Grades 1 and 2

In first and second grade, some of the writing that children will do for their main lesson books may involve copying what the teacher has written on the chalkboard. A teacher should not accept spelling errors in this type of writing. Stressing the importance of accurate copying encourages children to look carefully at words, a critical skill for developing proficient spelling.

If the teacher chooses, children in the early grades may periodically be given the opportunity to produce their own writing, perhaps about a story they have just heard or a common class experience. When children write on their own, they should have the confidence to spell phonetically how they hear the words. This will allow their writing to flow freely and render the writing process more enjoyable. A child who is very quick to ask how a word is spelled without trying first to spell it independently is less likely to develop proficient spelling. Even if children are not spelling all words correctly, they are doing a good job with this type of free writing if their spellings of words make sense. Invented spelling is acceptable in the early grades if a phonetically correct letter or set of letters represents each sound in the word.

It is not ever useful for a first or second grade class teacher to tell a child how to spell every word or to correct every spelling error in a child's own writing. Beginning in third grade, invented spelling should no longer be accepted, and correct spelling should be emphasized.

Assessment

Periodically in first and second grade, the teacher should give the class a spelling test to provide the teacher information about how to gear the spelling instruction. This type of spelling assessment may occur once every few months or as needed. For example, suppose that halfway through first grade, a class has been introduced to the alphabet but has not yet been given any CVC word spelling instruction, and they were then given a spelling test of ten different random CVC words. On this first assessment, a class as a whole may spell forty, fifty, sixty or even seventy percent of the CVC words correctly. Such a result would show that the class would benefit from spelling instruction with CVC words.

At the end of a language arts block in which the class has spent time practicing and learning to spell CVC words, the class may be assessed again. If the class as a whole, counting *all* spelling words the class spells correctly, receives above ninety percent, such result would show that the class has mastered the given stage of spelling. It is recommended that ninety percent be used as a cutoff because it shows that the children are spelling correctly with a high rate of success while also allowing some room for variability. It would not be reasonable to expect that on a single assessment every single child would achieve one hundred percent, but likewise, a teacher would not be challenging a class if the teacher were to settle for a lower percent. Ultimately, each class teacher and individual class circumstance will contribute to how any spelling assessment is used to inform the content of a teacher's future spelling lessons.

Grade 1

Learning Objectives:

- Children are able to rhyme and alliterate.

- Children are able to spell all CVC words correctly.

- During independent writing, children are able to break down words phonetically in order to produce spellings which make sense. It is acceptable if spelling is not correct.

- When children encounter unknown words while reading, they sound out the words phonetically and do not guess.

In the first half of first grade, children are introduced to the alphabet through images. Children should not only be able to look at a given letter and know what sound it makes (a skill required for reading), but they should also practice hearing the teacher say a sound and naming the correct letter (a skill required for spelling). From the beginning of first grade, the class benefits from work with alliteration and rhyming.

The main spelling-learning objective for first grade is that the children are able to hear the teacher say any CVC word, repeat the word, finger spell, and spell the word correctly. If the class is given adequate practice in the activities described previously, the final task of individually spelling the words correctly will come very easily to the children. When spelling individually, the teacher may remind the children to use finger spelling quietly to themselves for best results.

Grade 2

Learning Objectives:

- Children are able to rhyme and alliterate.

- Children are able to spell all CVC, CVCe, and consonant blend words heterogeneously.

- During independent writing, children are able to break down words phonetically in order to produce invented spellings which make sense. It is acceptable if spelling is not correct.

- When children reading encounter unknown words, they sound out the words phonetically and do not guess.

In second grade, the class continues with alliteration and rhyming work. Spelling instruction in second grade is similar in structure to the practices recommended for first grade. In second grade, children learn how to spell words that end with a silent "e." These words are known as CVCe (consonant-vowel-consonant-silent "e") words (e.g., *lake*, *hope*, etc.).

Once a class has mastered spelling CVCe words homogeneously, they may practice with CVCe and CVC words heterogeneously. Heterogeneous practice involves the teacher's using different CVC and CVCe words mixed throughout the lesson. Heterogeneous practice continues to refine children's listening capacity because they will not just automatically add a silent "e" to the end of every word, but rather, will have to listen for the long vowel sound in order to know when to add a silent "e."

In second grade, children are able to learn words with digraphs and consonant blends that include CCVC, CVCC, CCVCC, and CCVCe words. Although these words contain more letters, they are still regular words because they are spelled exactly as they sound. Some examples include: *flat* (CCVC), *lamp* (CVCC), *twist* (CCVCC), and *shape* (CCVCe). Practice with these words utilizes the skills that children mastered in learning the short and long vowel sounds in CVC and CVCe words. Children further their capacity for listening through identifying each consonant in a consonant blend. When finger spelling, each letter of a consonant blend should be represented with a separate finger.

During spelling instruction, a teacher should consistently be working from reading to spelling, whole-class questioning to individual questioning, and homogeneous to heterogeneous practice. By the end of second grade, if a class as a whole scores over ninety percent on a heterogeneous assessment of randomly assorted CVC, CVCe, and consonant blend words, the class is ready to begin learning pattern words in third grade. Either way, the class will benefit from sporadic continued practice with regular words heterogeneously with the new pattern words to come in grades 3 and 4.

Pattern Words – Grades 3, 4, 5 and 6

Beginning in third grade, children should start to use a balance of auditory and visual processing when learning spelling. Children can now learn to spell words that follow patterns or rules in our language. Spelling instruction with this focus meets children at this stage in their development by presenting them with words in which the spellings are based on social agreement. As the children become increasingly individual at the nine-year change, the teacher draws their attention to the importance of the social agreement necessary for spelling that allows people to communicate most easily.

Children will continue to use the careful listening they developed in the early grades in order to help them spell unknown words. They will begin to use careful looking as they visually store the spellings of easy words so they can be read automatically without being sounded out. Careful looking will allow children to recognize common spelling patterns that will further add to the number of words they are able to spell.

Introducing Patterns

A new pattern or rule is introduced to the class using a discovery method. The teacher presents a list of words, a poem, or an excerpt of writing that somehow emphasizes or draws attention to the spelling pattern the teacher wants to introduce. The teacher proceeds to ask the children what they notice about the words that make up the text selection. Some variability will result in children's responses as they creatively notice things the teacher had not intended, but ultimately the class will recognize the spelling pattern to be learned.

The class works together to develop a list of around ten words that use the same spelling pattern. If a list of ten cannot be developed, then the pattern is not common enough to be worth studying. If there are many more than ten words that can be found with the same pattern, still try to limit the list to ten. Ten is a useful number of words to focus on when teaching a new pattern; however, children can still be encouraged to independently discover words that contain the same pattern beyond the list of ten. Once a pattern has been learned and is being practiced heterogeneously with other patterns, the teacher should challenge the class by presenting new words containing the same pattern that were not on the class's original list of ten.

Sometimes it will occur that the same spelling pattern makes a different sound in two different words. In these cases, these two words should be included on the same spelling list because, in this stage of spelling development, the spelling of a word is more important than the sound. For example, the words *thread* and *treat* both contain the vowel pattern *ea*. In the word *thread*, the *ea* makes a short "e" sound while, in the word *treat*, the *ea* makes a long "e" sound. Two words such as these should be included on the same spelling list because they contain the same spelling pattern.

The introduction of a new spelling pattern does not always have to come intentionally from the teacher. The teacher and children may come across a word or group of words in their main lesson work or reading that contain an age-appropriate spelling pattern. The class may proceed to think of other words that use that same pattern in order to create a new spelling list for the class to study. To be clear: A single word from main lesson content may inspire a spelling list, but all of the challenging words used in a given main lesson block should not be made into a list and used for spelling instruction. A list of spelling words is most effective when it contains all words with the same spelling pattern. Recognition and explicit study of words with the same spelling pattern is what allows our brain to visually store the pattern so we can apply the pattern correctly in our writing.

Visualizing Words

When teaching words with spelling patterns, the importance of the visual component can be emphasized in a variety of ways.

- When writing spelling words on the chalkboard, the teacher uses a different color chalk when writing the letters of the spelling pattern.

- When spelling words are written on the chalkboard, the teacher erases only the letters in the spelling pattern, leaving the children to visualize what goes in the blank space.

- Children benefit from practice copying and writing their spelling words with their eyes closed when learning pattern words.

- As a the teacher standing in the front of the classroom, use a small personal chalkboard to flash a spelling word in front of the children for less than one second and have the children proceed to write and spell the word correctly. The children will be required to visualize how the words look and thus their ability to spell pattern words correctly will improve.

Activities such as these, which emphasize the visual component of learning spelling, are of importance in grades 3, 4, 5, and 6.

Many of the activities in this guide can be applied effectively in order to practice pattern words. Teachers should feel empowered to try out and practice activities of their own creation, while being guided by the criteria for effective spelling instruction, which include moving from reading to spelling, from whole-class questioning to individual questioning, and from homogeneous to heterogeneous practice. Prolonged homogeneous practice is even more important when teaching pattern words because if children are given heterogeneous practice too early and are not successful, they will be easily discouraged and confused by which patterns to apply at which times.

If necessary, multiple consecutive weeks can be dedicated to a single spelling pattern and a single list of approximately ten words. Although a period of one week is commonly used in schools for a single spelling list, one week may not be enough time to master a given spelling pattern. Overall, covering fewer spelling patterns and spending more time with each pattern is more beneficial than moving through many spelling patterns irrespective of student mastery.

Homonyms and Homophones

In grade 4, when teaching homonyms and homophones, the words should not be introduced in pairs, but rather taught first individually. For example, "there" and "their" should not be taught in the same lesson. First, "there" is taught and the children are given many opportunities to practice and understand how "there" is used correctly during several consecutive lessons. Then, "their" is taught and practiced. Finally, the children are ready to practice identifying whether "there" or "their" should be used in a given sentence. The study of a single pair of words, such as "there" and "their," may last for approximately a week or longer. Spending concentrated time on a single pair is more effective than studying a whole list of pairs all at once.

Writing in Grades 4, 5, 6 and 7

As children move through the grades, they increasingly produce more of their own writing for their main lesson books. Here, children can benefit from correcting their own spelling. When editing, the children should go through their work and underline any words that they think might be spelled incorrectly. For each word that has been underlined, the child should write down his or her three different best possible guesses as to how the word might be spelled and then choose the one amongst them that "looks right." The teacher should ultimately go through the children's writing and circle any words that are still spelled incorrectly, but have the children look up how to spell the word correctly. Children may also benefit by periodically editing each other's writing.

In addition to correcting their own writing, children should correct their own spelling assessments: tests and quizzes. This helps children learn from their own errors while also reducing grading time for the teacher. Ultimately, teachers will review tests and quizzes to help inform their instruction.

Homework

Appropriate spelling practice involves having the children write the given spelling words three times each. If children are called to write a word more than three times, the work becomes tedious and not useful towards spelling development. Additionally, practice of this type gives children an opportunity to work on their cursive handwriting skills.

If a teacher notices in a child's writing that words are being misspelled that contain spelling patterns that the class has already studied explicitly, the teacher may assign individualized homework that will ask the child to find as many words as possible that have the same spelling pattern as the misspelled word. Homework of this type is not intended as punishment, but is genuinely useful in helping the child learn how to correctly apply the spelling pattern.

Grade 3

Learning Objectives:

- Children are able to spell words with common consonant and vowel patterns heterogeneously with the regular words learned in grades 1 and 2.

- Children are able to edit their own spelling errors by seeing if a word "looks right."

- When children encounter unknown words while reading, they sound out the words phonetically and do not guess.

- When children encounter short and common words while reading, they know the words quickly and automatically without having to sound them out.

In third grade, children should study explicitly the most common consonant patterns and vowel patterns. Vowel patterns often occur in the CVVC form, and some patterns that may be studied in third grade are *ai, ay, ei, ea, ee, ie, oa, oo,* and *ow*. Spelling instruction in third grade should follow the recommended practices described for teaching pattern words.

Spelling instruction for teaching a single pattern should involve a short amount of practice each day for consecutive weeks using the most applicable activities. The children discover the pattern to be studied and together develop a list of words with the same pattern. The activities focus on visualization and each day progress from reading to spelling, whole-class to individual, and homogeneous to heterogeneous practice. Heterogeneous practice may involve words learned in the early grades as well as the new pattern words being learned.

Grade 4

Learning Objectives:

- Children are able to apply spelling rules for adding endings to words for different tenses.

- Children are able to spell and use common homonyms and homophones correctly in their writing.

- Children are able to spell words with common vowel patterns heterogeneously with the regular words learned in grades 1 and 2.

- Children are able to edit their own spelling errors by seeing if a word "looks right."

- When children encounter unknown words while reading, they sound out the words phonetically and do not guess.

- When children encounter short and common words while reading, they know the words quickly and automatically without having to sound them out.

In fourth grade, children should learn rules for conjugating verbs into different tenses. They learn how to add *-s, -ed*, and *-ing* to the end of words. Rules are different from spelling patterns in that they do not just occur frequently, but they are always followed in every case. Fourth graders may study homonyms, homophones, and common writing and spelling errors such as *there, their, they're; to, too, two;* and *its, it's.* Spelling instruction in fourth grade should follow the recommended practices described for teaching pattern words.

Spelling instruction for teaching rules and common errors should involve a short amount of practice each day for consecutive weeks using the most applicable activities. The children discover the rule to be studied. The activities each day focus on visualization and progress from reading to spelling, whole-class to individual, and homogeneous to heterogeneous practice.

Grades 5 and 6

Learning Objectives:

- Children are able to spell words with more complex patterns including prefixes and suffixes.

- Children are able to spell and know the meanings of words containing Greek and Latin roots.

- Children are able to correctly apply some more sophisticated writing errors such as affect/effect and farther/further.

- Children are able to edit their own spelling errors by seeing if a word "looks right."

At this stage in their development, children are beginning to develop abstract thinking. In fifth and sixth grade, children learn words with Greek and Latin roots and more complex patterns including prefixes and suffixes. Words with Greek and Latin roots get their meanings from abstract concepts that are separate from the nature of the sounds and social convention; for this reason, these words meet the consciousness of fifth and sixth graders. Spelling instruction should follow the recommended practices described for teaching pattern words.

Irregular Words – Grades 7 and 8

By grades 7 and 8, children who have been taught spelling through the aforementioned practices will likely be very good spellers. At this final stage of spelling development, children learn how to spell irregular words. Learning irregular words requires a heavy reliance on visual processing in order to store and access the correct spellings of these words. The effective practices related to spelling practice, spelling tests, and editing used during grades 3 through 6 should still be consistently applied throughout grades 7 and 8. At this point, because spelling words are irregular, they may come from main lesson content or students' reading and writing.

If a student in the later grades is not a proficient speller, it is likely because he has yet to master one or more of the previous stages of spelling development. At this point, a teacher may assess what types of errors the student makes and with what types of words the student needs more practice. Through individualized instruction, a teacher with an understanding of spelling development will be able to meet any student at his or her current ability level and help that student move toward proficient spelling.

Spelling Curriculum Summary Grades 1-6

Grade/Age	Developmental Need	Stage of Spelling Development
1 / 7	Present the children with words in which the spellings make sense. As a result, the children learn that the world is a safe and sensible place, as opposed to the randomness and uncertainty they may experience if exposed to more challenging spelling words.	Regular words – words that are spelled exactly as they sound
2 / 8		
3 / 9	Present the children with words in which the spellings are based on social agreement. As the children become increasingly individual at the nine-year change, draw their attention to the importance of the social agreement necessary for spelling as it allows people to communicate most easily.	Pattern words – words that are not spelled exactly as they sound and that contain a pattern of letters that repeats in many different words
4 / 10		
5 / 11	Children are increasingly able to begin developing abstract thinking. Words with Greek and Latin roots derive their meanings from abstract concepts that are separate from the nature of the sounds and social convention.	
6 / 12		Irregular words – words that are not spelled exactly as they sound and that have parts that do not contain a common pattern

Capacity	New Types of Words Introduced	Sample Words	Classroom Activities and Key Practices
Listening, auditory	CVC	hat, red, mix top, cup	-Rhyme -Alliterate -Finger spelling -Invented spelling -Sound cards -Movement and rhythm
	Silent e Consonant blends CVCC, CCVC, CCVCC	lake, wide, flute, poke, jump, skip, blond, chop, wish, think, luck	
Listening and looking, auditory and visual	Common consonant patterns Common vowel patterns – CVVC	white, knit, high, sting, sketch, fudge, speed, book, clay, enjoy	-Discovery method -Lists of ten words -Visualizing activities -Editing based on what "looks right" -Correct spelling -Introduce a common error pair one word at a time -Practice three times each -Students grade their own assessments
	Vowel patterns, tenses, common writing errors – homophones, homonyms	again, hawk, bowl, weather, toast, avoid, sound, there/their/they're	
	Greek roots Common prefixes		
	Latin roots Common suffixes Sophisticated writing errors		

Spelling Activities and Games

The following spelling activities and games include some that were presented earlier in this guide and more that have not yet been mentioned. Some of the activities offer direct spelling practice while others may simply offer children opportunities to play with words in new ways. The classroom activities recommended in this guide are described in a straightforward way in order to give the teacher a clear idea of the spelling skill that requires practicing. It is developmentally appropriate, particularly in the early grades, for a creative teacher to introduce and guide a spelling practice activity into a story or a game in order to meet the children so long as the imagination does not distract or deter from the spelling work.

The activities are listed generally in grade order with the most appropriate first-grade activities first; however, many of the activities can be adapted to match the rigor required at any grade level and therefore grade level recommendations are not given. Dedicating a short amount of main lesson time each day to repetitive spelling instruction that moves from reading to spelling, whole-class questioning to individual questioning, and homogeneous to heterogeneous practice will result in students who spell proficiently and love language.

Activities and Games List

Alliteration – The children identify as many words as possible that begin or end with a given sound. A sponge mop can be used to draw a letter on the blackboard and the class can see how many words beginning or ending with that letter can be named before the letter disappears.

Alliterative speech exercises help to reinforce the sound of a letter, For example, "Round and round the rugged rock the ragged rascal ran."
or   "Little Miss Munching Mouse munches mincemeat in my house.
  Lamp or light no longer lit,
  Munching nibbling bit by bit—bits of bread and beads and buns,
  Comes the cat, to catch the crumbs."

Rhyming – The children identify as many words as possible that rhyme with a given word.

Beginning, Middle, End – The children identify whether a given sound occurs in the beginning, middle, and/or end of a word. A paragraph from a familiar story is written on the blackboard and a child or the class finds all of the same letter occurring in it.

Counting Sounds – The children listen to the teacher speak a sentence and count how many of a given sound they hear.

Letter Cards – The teacher has large pieces of white cardboard with a different letter or spelling pattern written on each one. The teacher shows a given card to a child and the child says the sound that the letter or spelling pattern makes in a word.

Spoken Sounds – The children stand in a row at their desks. The teacher says a sound of a letter or spelling pattern being studied. The child says the name of the letter or spelling pattern that makes that sound. The child sits down.

Reading with Finger Spelling – Words are written in a list on the chalkboard. The children say a given word, and then using finger spelling, separate and say the sound made by each letter, and say the given word again.

Listening with Finger Spelling – The teacher says a word. The children finger spell the word.

Spelling Aloud with Finger Spelling – The teacher spells a word aloud. The children say and finger spell the word aloud. Or a child spells a spelling word in front of the class and calls on another child to pronounce it correctly. The responding child finger spells, says the word, and then takes a turn to stand in front of the class and spell a new word.

Individual Chalkboards – Each child has an individual chalkboard, chalk, and eraser. The teacher says a word. The children spell the word on their chalkboard. The children are reminded to silently finger spell the word to themselves in order to figure out how to spell it. An individual child is called on to finger spell and actually spell the word so the other children can check if they were correct.

Individual Sets of Letter Cards – Each child creates his or her own set of small cards that have a single letter of the alphabet on each. The children spell words by arranging their cards on their desks. One benefit of creating these cards is that it frees the children from the task of writing that may require too much concentrated attention in the early grades.

Charades – The teacher gives a group of children a word to spell using the shapes of their bodies to create the shapes of each letter in the word. In grade 1, a single letter can be used. The class identifies the correct word or letter, and a new group of children is selected.

Spelling on Back or Palm – Children spell words by writing letters on each other's back or palm with their finger.

Spelling in the Air – The teacher writes a word with a finger in the air in front of the class, and the children identify the word.

Spelling with Feet – Children take off their shoes, place the pencil between their toes, and write with their feet.

Spelling with Different Materials – Children spell words on their desks or on the floor using the material provided (e.g., stones, shells, twigs, beeswax, gems, pipe cleaners, toothpicks, etc.)

Simon Says Sounds – The teacher says a word and assigns a certain activity for the children to do when they hear a given sound in a word. For example, when a class is studying CVC words, and the teacher says a random CVC word, if the word has the short "a" sound, the children clap above their head. If the word has a short "i" sound, the children stand up. If the word has a short "u" sound, the children stomp their feet, etc.

First to Last – A child says a word and the next child says a word that begins with the same letter or sound that the previous child's word ended with, and this pattern continues. This game can be played with spelling words or words of a certain category such as animals or food.

Rhythm and Movement – Children spell words aloud to a song or rhythm and/or accompany it with a movement such as jumping rope, bouncing a ball, tossing a bean bag, hopping, or clapping.

Add a Letter – The first child in a row says the name of any letter. The next child says any letter to become the next letter in the word being spelled. This process is repeated until a word is spelled. The word being spelled should come from the spelling words that the class is currently studying. The last child finger spells and says the word. The process is repeated with the next row of children. Or, instead of the word being spelled being unknown initially, the teacher chooses a word and asks the children in a row to say a single letter each until the word is spelled.

Clues for Rhyme – The teacher thinks of two words that rhyme (e.g., *bat, cat*). The teacher thinks of a single clue for each of the rhyming words (e.g., the clue for *bat* could be *baseball* and the clue for *cat* could be *dog*). The teacher says the clues (e.g., *baseball, dog*) and the children figure out the corresponding rhyming words (e.g., *bat, cat*) knowing that the words they are guessing rhyme.

Snowman – This is a variation of the common game, "Hangman." The teacher or a child has a word in mind for which they write blank spaces and draw a snowman on the chalkboard. The remaining children guess letters in order to try and figure out the word. As incorrect letters are guessed, different parts of the snowman melt away (are erased).

Nonsense Spelling – The teacher says a nonsense word, usually in the form of CCVCC, that is spelled exactly how it sounds, and asks the children to spell the word correctly. This activity is useful for teaching child to rely on their careful listening

Three Times Each – Children use their best cursive handwriting to write their spelling words three times each.

Spelling in Step – Children write their spelling words by adding one letter to each line until the word has been spelled completely. Then, starting from the beginning of the completed word, each letter can be subtracted and the results written in the same way:

B	Boat
Bo	oat
Boa	at
Boat	t

Spelling in Different Sizes – Children write their spelling words three times each: once big, once medium, and then once as small as they can, all on the same line on the same page.

Meaningful Homework – A student takes a misspelled word from class writing and, for homework, attempts to write many other different words that have the same spelling pattern and series of letters which the student misspelled in them.

Word Finder – The children look through an age-appropriate book for as many words as possible with particular vowel patterns that have been studied. The words that the children come up with can be used in future class spelling practice or the children can produce a poem using a concentrated number of words with the same spelling pattern.

Eyes Closed – The spelling words are written on the chalkboard. The children look at each word in turn, close their eyes, and then write the word on their page while their eyes are still closed. The class proceeds on future days to spell with their eyes closed without looking at the words beforehand. This activity emphasizes the importance of the visual component required for spelling pattern words.

Speedy – Flash a word in front of the students incredibly quickly (using large paper, the chalkboard, or a projector) and see if the students can read the word after only seeing it for less than a second. This activity emphasizes the importance of the visual component required for spelling pattern words.

Using the Words – Children write a story, poem, or sentences using their spelling words.

Editing – The teacher writes a passage on the chalkboard with words that have been intentionally spelled incorrectly. The children identify the spelling errors. Or, the teacher writes a list of many words on the chalkboard, with only some them spelled incorrectly, and the children identify the incorrectly spelled words.

Unscramble – The teacher scrambles the letters of spelling words and writes them on the chalkboard. The children unscramble the words.

Spelling Spree – Each child begins with a piece of paper and pencil. The teacher starts everyone with the same word and asks the children to generate new words by changing, adding, or subtracting one letter at a time for five minutes in order to see who can create the most words (e.g., "plan" – *plane, play, place, plate, plans, pan, pane, panes, planet, plea*, etc.)

Tea Kettle – Create a sentence with two homophones in it and substitute the words "tea kettle" for the homophone. Have the students identify which correct homophone goes where in the sentence.

Homophone Riddles – Think of a clever way to connect the correct meanings of two homophones and develop a question that would create the homophones as the answer to the riddle. For example, "Why did the window go to the doctor? He had pane pain."

Spelling Word Lists

Rhyming Fun

Words for which children will easily be able to find many rhymes

cat	cap	back	pen	best	sit
pin	hill	lip	ink	top	hot
lock	bug	jump	duck	lake	game
skate	night	king	mail	rain	day
paw	snow	eat	sheep		

Regular Words

CVC

bat	cap	cat	dad	fat	hag
had	has	hat	lad	lap	mat
map	pal	pat	nap	rat	sap
sat	tap	wag	wax		

bed	beg	bet	den	get	hem
hen	jet	leg	let	men	met
net	red	set	ten	vet	vex
peg	pen	pet	web	wet	

big	bin	bit	did	dig	dim
din	dip	fib	fig	fin	fit
fix	hid	him	hip	hit	kid
kit	mix	lid	lip	lit	pig
pin	pit	rib	rid	rim	rip
sin	sip	sit	tin	tip	wig
win	wit				

box	cot	fog	fox	dog	dot
got	hop	hot	job	jog	lob
log	lot	not	nod	pop	pot
mob	mom	mop	rod	rot	sob
top					

bud	bug	bun	bus	cub	cup
cut	dug	fun	gut	gum	hug
hut	jug	lug	mug	mud	nut
sun	tub	pup			

Bat, cat, fat, mat, rat, pat, sat
Wet, vet, set, bet, get, met, let, net
Den, ten, pen, men, hen
Rot, cot, pot, hot, not
Bug, dug, mug, rug, lug, jug, hug
Bit, fit, hit, kit, lit, pit, sit, wit
Bin, din, fin, pin, sin, win

Tap, tip, top
Pen, pin
Beg, big, bug
Pat, pet, pit, pot
Hat, hit, hot, hut
Bat, bet, bit, but
Sat, set, sit

Consonant Blend Words

CVCC

lamp	vast	camp	damp	raft	
vest	mesh	wept	dent	rent	desk
list	sift	wisp	wish		
fond					
jump	dust	much	hunt	hush	

41

CCVC

glad	flat	flap			
fled	step	them			
skid	drip	ship	skip	shin	grin
stop	drop	trot	spot	slot	flop
shut	stub	spun	stun		

CCVCC

grasp	grant	clamp	slash	clasp	stand
dwelt	crest	chest	slept	spent	blend
twist	brisk	flint	blink	swift	crisp
blond	stomp				
crust	stump	slump	plump	blush	slush

Nonsense CCVCC

chast					
chemp	quelt	chent	clemp	stelk	
slimp	stimp	blist	chilk	flish	crift
shilk	plimp	slint	slish		
flosh	twost	flont	sholf	swoft	crosp
pront					
cruft	gruth	slunt	blust		

Silent E Words

Words to add e to the end in order to make silent e words

can	cane		sit	site
tap	tape		slim	slime
man	mane		rob	robe
cap	cape		hop	hope
pin	pine		cub	cube
kit	kite		tub	tube

Silent E

a-e

bake	base	cage	cake	cane	came
cape	case	cave	chase	date	
faze	face	fade	fake	flake	
gate	gave	gaze	hate	haze	
lake	lame	lane	late		
made	make	mane	maze	name	
pace	page	pave	plane		
race	rage	rake	rate	rave	
sage	sake	same	save	shape	snake
space	take	tame	tape		

e-e

these	theme	here

i-e

dice	mice	nice	rice	hide	ride
wide	life	time	mile	pile	bike
hike	like	fine	line	nine	vine
side	lime	dime	wipe	pipe	kite
bite	glide	sprite	prize	slide	smile
wise	fire	wire	ice	five	

o-e

hope	home	woke	joke	bone	slope
stove	robe	rode	rope	nose	rose
poke	pole	note	vote		

u-e

mute	cute	cube	cure	rule	flute
prune	June	tune	huge	yube	

Pattern Words

Common Consonant Patterns

ch

chin	chop	chest	chug	inch	much
rich	lunch				

sh

shop	shed	shift	wish	dash	crush
rush	flash				

th

thin	thick	think	that	this	third
bath	path				

wh

why	what	whip	when	whim	whale
white	whisper				

kn

knit	knee	knelt	knife	knob	know
knight					

ck

back	duck	luck	kick	neck	pack
black	block	shack	click		

gh

high	sigh	eight	weigh	night	cough
dough	light	ghost	thigh	right	

ng

ring	sing	thing	sting	hung	swung
clang	string				

tch

match	patch	sketch	fetch	clutch	crutch
witch	stitch				

dge

badge	wedge	fudge	judge	ridge	nudge
ledge					

ph

phone	phase	photograph	elephant	philosophy
paragraph	pharmacy	triumph	phenomenon	

Common Vowel Patterns

ai

fail	jail	maid	paid	said	wait
rain	daisy	faint	mail	grain	
air	chair	dairy	fair	pair	hair

aw

draw	yawn	lawn	saw	paw	claw
dawn	straw	raw	hawk		

ay

say	may	play	day	stay	sway
clay	way	stray	payment	crayon	hay
crayon					

ea

head	bread	weather			
deal	team	clean	seat	beach	mean

ee

bee	need	speed	tree	queen	sweet
sweep	sheep	three	teeth	squeeze	cheer

oa

boat	coat	coal	goal	toad	soap
toast	oak	loaf	coast		

oi

oil	boil	join	coin	noise	avoid
spoil	soil	point	voice		

oo

book	cook	hook	good	hood	wood
food	hook	bloom	proof	zoo	too
choose	mushroom	balloon	childhood		

ou

loud	sound	found	shout	count	about
cloud	couch	flour	doubt		
touch					

ow

cow	how	owl	now	down
bowl	glow	know	owe	show

oy

toy	joy	boy	annoy	loyal	enjoy
decoy					

Tenses – Adding Endings

watch	watches	watched	watching		
taste	tastes	tasted	tasting		
finish	finishes	finished	finishing		
skip	miss	relax	laugh	try	jump
explore	fuss	drip	worry		

Common Errors

there	their	they're
to	too	two
are	our	hour
your	you're	
its	it's	
no	know	
whether	weather	
whose	who's	

Sophisticated Errors

than	then
affect	effect
accept	except
compliment	complement
farther	further
discrete	discreet
foreword	forward
lose	loose
good	well
past	passed
that	which
who	whom
e.g.	i.e.

Common Prefixes

Prefix	Definition	Example
anti-	against	anticlimax
de-	opposite	devalue
dis-	not; opposite of	discover
en-, em-	cause to	enact, empower
fore-	before; front of	foreshadow, forearm
in-, im-	in	income, impulse
in-, im-, il-, ir-	not	indirect, immoral, illiterate, irreverent
inter-	between; among	interrupt
mid-	middle	midfield
mis-	wrongly	misspell
non-	not	nonviolent
over-	over; too much	overeat
pre-	before	preview
re-	again	rewrite
semi-	half; partly; not fully	semifinal
sub-	under	subway
super-	above; beyond	superhuman
trans-	across	transmit
un-	not; opposite of	unusual
under-	under; too little	underestimate

Reproduced with permission from Corwin Press.

Common Suffixes

Suffix	Definition	Example
-able, -ible	is; can be	affordable, sensible
-al, -ial	having characteristics of	universal, facial
-ed	past tense verbs; adjectives	the dog walked, the walked dog
-en	made of	golden
-er, -or	one who; person connected with	teacher, professor
-er	more	taller
-est	the most	tallest
-ful	full of	helpful
-ic	having characteristics of	poetic
-ing	verb forms; present participles	sleeping
-ion, -tion, -ation, -ition	act; process	submission, motion, relation, edition
-ity, -ty	state of	activity, society
-ive, -ative, -itive	adjective form of noun	active, comparative, sensitive
-less	without	hopeless
-ly	how something is	lovely
-ment	state of being; act of	contentment
-ness	state of; condition of	openness
-ous, -eous, -ious	having qualities of	riotous, courageous, gracious
-s, -es	more than one	trains, trenches
-y	characterized by	gloomy

Reproduced with permission from Corwin Press.

Root Words, Roots and Affixes

Familiarity with Greek and Latin roots, as well as prefixes and suffixes, can help students understand the meanings of new words. Recognizing Greek word patterns and their meanings can also help the students spell many new words. Many English words are formed by taking basic words and adding either a prefix or a suffix to them. A basic word to which affixes (prefixes and suffixes) are added is called a *root word* because it forms the basis of a new word. The root word is often a word in its own right. For example, the word *lovely* consists of the word *love* and the suffix *-ly*.

In contrast, a *root* is not typically a stand-alone word. For example, the word *reject* is made from the prefix *re-* and the Latin root *ject*, which is not a stand-alone word.

While the following lists of Greek and Latin roots include many common examples, they are not comprehensive. But this will give you a good start.

Common Greek Roots

Greek Root	Definition	Example
anthropo	man; human; humanity	anthropologist, philanthropy
auto	self	autobiography, automobile
bio	life	biology, biography
chron	time	chronological, chronic
dyna	power	dynamic, dynamite
dys	bad; hard; unlucky	dysfunctional, dyslexic
gram	thing written	epigram, telegram
graph	writing	graphic, phonograph
hetero	different	heteronym, heterogeneous
homo	same	homonym, homogenous
hydr	water	hydration, dehydrate
hyper	over; above; beyond	hyperactive, hyperbole
hypo	below; beneath	hypothermia, hypothetical
logy	study of	biology, psychology
meter/metr	measure	thermometer, metronome
micro	small	microbe, microscope
mis/miso	hate	misanthrope, misogyny
mono	one	monologue, monotonous
morph	form; shape	morphology, morphing
nym	name	antonym, synonym
phil	love	philanthropist, philosophy
phobia	fear	claustrophobia, phobic
photo/phos	light	photograph, phosphorous

pseudo	false	pseudonym, pseudoscience
psycho	soul; spirit	psychology, psychic
scope	viewing instrument	microscope,
techno	art; science; skill	technique, technology
tele	far off	television, telephone
therm	heat	thermal, thermometer

Note: Many Greek roots spell the /f/ sound with the letters *ph*. When you hear the /f/ sound in an unfamiliar word with a Greek root, spell it with a *ph*.

Common Latin Roots

Latin Root	Definition	Example
ambi	both	ambiguous, ambidextrous
aqua	water	aquarium, aquamarine
aud	to hear	audience, audition
bene	good	benefactor, benevolent
cent	one hundred	century, percent
circum	around	circumference, circumstance
contra/counter	against	contradict, encounter
dict	to say	dictation, dictator
duc/duct	to lead	conduct, induce
fac	to do; to make	factory, manufacture
form	shape	conform, reform
fort	strength	fortitude, fortress
fract	break	fracture, fraction
ject	throw	projection, rejection
jud	judge	judicial, prejudice
mal	bad	malevolent, malefactor
mater	mother	maternal, maternity
mit	to send	transmit, admit
mort	death	mortal, mortician
multi	many	multimedia, multiple
pater	father	paternal, paternity
port	to carry	portable, transportation
rupt	to break	bankrupt, disruption

scrib/script	to write	inscription, prescribe
sect/sec	to cut	bisect, section
sent	to feel; to send	consent, resent
spect	to look	inspection, spectator
struct	to build	destruction, restructure
vid/vis	to see	televise, video
voc	voice; to call	vocalize, advocate

Bibliography

Burkhardt, Sally E. (2011). *Using the brain to spell: Effective strategies for all levels*. United Kingdom: Rowman & Littlefield Publishers.

Carreker, Suzanne, ed. Judith R. Birsh. (1999). *Multisensory teaching of basic language skills: Teaching spelling*. Baltimore, MD: Paul H. Brookes Publishing Co.

Dean, John F. (1956). *Games make spelling fun*. Palo Alto, CA: Fearon Publishers.

Forte, Imogene and Mary Ann Pangle. (1976). *Spelling magic: Activities, gimmicks, games galore for making learning mean lots more!!* Nashville, TN: Incentive Publications.

Gentry, Richard J. (2004). *The science of spelling: The explicit strategies that make great readers and writers (and spellers!)*. Portsmouth, NH: Heinemann.

Johnson, Susan R. (2007). *You and your child's health: Teaching your child how to read, write, and spell*. www.youandyourchildshealth.org.

Marten, Cindy. (2003). *Word crafting: Teaching spelling, grades K–6*. Portsmouth, NH: Heinemann.

Monges. Lisa D. (1964). "Making spelling a lively experience." *Education as an Art*, Vol. 24, No. 1.

Pusch, Ruth. (1964). "Spelling lessons." *Education as an Art*, Vol. 24, No. 1.

Steiner, Rudolf. (1995). *The genius of language: observations for teachers*. Great Barrington, MA: Anthroposophic Press.

Steiner, Rudolf, ed. Roberto Trostli. (2004). *Teaching language arts in the Waldorf school: A compendium of excerpts from the Foundations of Waldorf Education series*. Fair Oaks, CA: AWSNA Publications.

Thirty True Tales of the
Weird, Unusual and Macabre

FROM THE NOTEBOOKS OF THE PARANORMAL JOURNALIST

PAT BUSSARD

REAPER PUBLISHING
LEBANON, VIRGINIA

REAPER PUBLISHING

ℛ

Lebanon, VA 24266

ISBN-13: 978-0615796857
ISBN-10: 0615796850 (pbk.)

Printed in the United States of America.

Contents

Acknowledgements

MY greatest debt is to my grandmother and mother, Lennie and Alice Roberts, the two women who taught me the value of the written word. They gave me an eclectic upbringing unbound by the chains of the mundane, where fairies danced in magic circles, witches did not have green faces, ghosts were just interesting people, and my imagination could soar through universes. I miss you both.

To my sisters Pam Wilson Roberts and Tracey Piazza, you are my heart and your belief in me and support means so much. Together, we have the power of three.

To the rest of my family including my lovely daughters Stephanie, Megan, and niece Morgan, thank you for your support.

My oldest friend Marty Workman inspires me to keep seeking out the fantastic worlds that reside within the pages of books. She is like one of the characters in the fantasy novels she reads, having the mind of a poet and the heart of a warrior.

For graciously writing the foreword for *The Paranormal Journalist*, I would like to thank renowned author Rosemary Ellen Guiley. I am humbled that in spite of her heavy writing schedule, she found time to contribute to the most important writing project of my life thus far.

Thank you all!

Foreword

DID you ever have an experience that challenged your view of reality? Maybe you saw a ghost or a mysterious light moving about the sky. Perhaps you had a dream that came true. Or, perhaps you saw a "creature" that did not seem to belong to this world. At first, you might have passed it off as imagination, a trick of light, or something natural and explainable – and much to your awe or discomfort, you came up empty-handed.

Strange things do happen on our planet – ghosts, hauntings, weird lights and shadows, mysterious entities and more. Everyone at some point has an experience with the Unknown, something that just cannot be explained naturally.

If you're like most people, you find the paranormal at once intriguing and maybe a little bit scary. Or a lot scary! Where do you go to learn more?

Pat Bussard has the answer with her engaging collection of articles about some of the most popular topics in the paranormal – the real deal, not the fictions in novels, television and film. She will introduce you to real ghosts, vampires, werewolves, aliens, frightening creatures, prophecy, witchcraft, and what it's like to do investigations of haunted places. throughout, she presents an objective, balanced picture – the provable and the unprovable, but nonetheless probable.

Most of the paranormal consists of the unproven, except through millions of personal experiences. Human beings have had paranormal experiences throughout history that have been fairly consistent throughout the ages, even though our explanations change with culture, science, technology, and the advancement of knowledge. Science and religion, the two institutions to which most people turn when it comes to the paranormal, have limited abilities to address all angles of it. The paranormal defies all the standards of science, and so many scientists refuse to examine it at all. Religion has its own agenda. Neither is right nor wrong, but the answers lie somewhere in between, in a truth for every individual to figure out for himself or herself.

In my own career as a paranormal researcher, investigator and author – which began in the 1980s – I have always wanted to know as much as I can about all aspects of it. My paranormal quest to know about everything was driven by my own curiosity, but I soon realized a greater purpose to it. Early on I saw that phenomena and experiences are all interconnected, sometimes dramatically, sometimes subtly. I have always urged people who are interested in the paranormal to study as much as they can about as many subjects as possible. We can't be expert in everything, of course, but in order to understand the big picture, we have to pull far back and see all the pieces – not just a few of them.

I have had quite an adventure, which in turn has reshaped my perception of reality, and what goes on around us without us being aware of it most of the time. I have stretched my own sense of what is possible "out there." Nearly three decades of investigations and personal experiences of my own have convinced me that paranormal phenomena are indeed real, that other worlds lie beyond ours in layers of dimensions, and we are capable of interacting with a variety of spirits and beings and even bending space and time.

Things we think are only imagination are instead real and can happen to anyone – perhaps even you. Strange dimensions lie right next to ours, and doorways open all time to reveal the secrets of other worlds. For example, if you thought vampires cannot possibly exist outside of a novel or a Hollywood film, read about them here and you may find yourself revising your thinking.

Pat Bussard's collection of topics in this volume offers an excellent introduction to many of the mysterious and exciting phenomena of the paranormal realm – things you have wondered about, things you may have already encountered yourself, or might at some time in the future. I have journalism training and experience in my background, and so I appreciate Pat's straightforward reporting on these subjects, and her ability to carry the reader into a journey of discovery. When it comes to the paranormal, truth really is stranger than fiction!

Vampires, ghosts, the Djinn, Mothman, UFOs and other subjects in this book are genuine – not like the entertainment industry dishes them out, but very real indeed, and our ancestors dealt with them as we are dealing with them. When we are in the right place at the right time, the doors between worlds swing open.

Rosemary Ellen Guiley
Author, *The Encyclopedia of Ghosts & Spirits*

the theatre, including those by Master Magician MacDonald Birch (1902 – 1992), a McConnelsville native. This world famous slight-of-hand wizard, worked at the opera house when he was only a boy before embarking on his journey to conquer the world's most prestigious stages. His job then was to light the gaslight chandeliers. He was inspired to go into show business when he watched acts perform by peeking through the taper holes near the chandelier.

Inside the Twin City Opera House.

Birch eventually went on to command the attention of audiences and the respect of his contemporaries such as the great magicians Houdini, Thurston, and Blackstone. Birch was best known for his vanishing pony and Silk Mirage acts, as well as his suave good looks. His stint at the Opera House must have left an impression on Birch, as he is reported to have returned to his old haunt.

One paranormal research team has encountered Birch and the additional otherworldly inhabitants of the theatre on a regular basis. Eric Glosser is the director of the United Paranormal Project (UPP). He grew up with an interest in the paranormal, listening to the stories his mother would share with him. Because of this early introduction to the preternatural, Glosser grew up wanting to be a parapsychologist. Life, however, had a different plan for him and after spending 23 years in law enforcement and another 12 as an instructor in the police academy he retired. "After retiring, I found that I had to do something to keep my mind occupied," said Glosser. "After thinking it over, I realized that it was time for me to go into paranormal investigating. In 2007 I joined a team and within a few months I became the case manager and within a year I was promoted to director. In February of 2011, I along with all of my members decided to broaden our paranormal boundaries and goals by starting the United Paranormal Project. We are Ohio representatives of The American Ghost Society founded by Troy

Taylor," said Glosser. They now investigate numerous private residences, as well as a few high profile locations.

Glosser has also produced and directed six paranormal documentary films to date and is currently working on the seventh. Two of the films, through his film production company Paraeglo Films, feature the theatre's spirits. Those titles are "The Phantoms of the Twin City Opera House," and "The Ghosts' of the Opera House."

"I witnessed many strange things in my years as a police officer that could not be explained," said Glosser. He continued, "These occurrences even strengthened my desire to understand the paranormal. There are so many things that we don't know. Occasionally, when I am lucky enough to answer a question about the paranormal, it just opens up another door with a hundred new questions."

The other members of Glosser's research team include: Marty Myers, public relations manager; Brendan Shay, tech manager; Amy Fortney, case manager; Meg Work, investigator; Jessica Work, investigator; Michaela Hartley, investigator; and Martha Whittington, investigator.

Glosser and his team have investigated the Opera House for years. "I contacted Adam Shriver, the executive director of the theatre, in early 2008 to find out how my team could gain access to the location in order to conduct an investigation. His dad, Rick Shriver, is president of the board of the non-profit organization dedicated to preserving the opera house. We investigated there twice within a few months and were amazed at the amount of paranormal activity that took place," said Glosser. After investigating the Twin City Opera House, Glosser asked if Shriver would let them manage all of the paranormal functions there and they have been successfully doing so ever since. In just over three years, over fifty paranormal investigative teams from across the United States have performed private investigations at the theatre.

Glosser also manages all of the paranormal functions at another haunted Ohio location, the Bryn Du Mansion.

The theatre, however, is a special place for Glosser and the other members of UPP. Over the years he and his team have made the acquaintance of each of the fourteen reported spirits that dwell within the opera house that H.C. Lindsay, an architect from Zanesville, Ohio, designed. "My favorite of the spirits, hands down, is Robert 'Red Wine Lowery.' He was a former stage hand back at the turn of the century. He haunts the catwalk and is very active. We have captured Robert saying, 'I've got red wine,' on two different occasions," said Glosser. He continued, "Robert is very much like me, in that he likes to joke around. I think this is why we get along so well. Even if he is not communicating with groups when they are investigating, if they ask me to go up to see if I can get him to cooperate, within minutes he responds."

MacDonald Birch and Robert Lowery are only two of the ghostly residents of the Twin City Opera House. Glosser and the UPP team, as a result of years of research and eyewitness claims report a dozen more:

- Elizabeth, a ten year old girl, whose mother was a performer at the opera house in the early 1900s. She also haunts the catwalk and may have known Robert Lowery during her lifetime. The UPP team has a clear recording of Elizabeth saying, "I forgive."

- Everett Miller, an usher at the opera house for thirty years. His apparition is seen roaming the aisles of the auditorium. His name has also been captured on audio recording devices.
- The "White Victorian Lady," a woman in white Victorian garb, seen many times crossing the stage and walking up the stairs, onto the catwalk, and then into an old dressing room. Her spirit lights up the stage during her appearances and causes the temperature to drastically drop.
- Charlie, a very strong presence that seldom associates with the UPP team.

Two members of The Ghost Writers paranormal investigative team pictured on a haunted stairwell in the Opera House.

Those who interact with Charlie can expect to feel nauseous and to feel severe temperature drops.

- Sara, a 12 year old girl with whom the team has made contact. She appears in the old coat rack room, just off the ballroom on the third floor. Sara is very selective with whom she speaks.
- John Leezer, a man who was fatally stabbed in the third floor ballroom around 1905. Many have felt his presence in the room. According to the UPP team and other witnesses, John has dropped the temperature and has even gone "through" an investigator causing nausea and cold chills.
- "Black Shadow Man," has been seen a number of times. He is usually

The third floor ballroom where John Leezer was fatally stabbed in 1905.

spotted walking down the far left aisle of the theatre and then walking up the stairs before entering the left side of the stage area. This spirit wears a dark cowboy style hat and a long duster or trench style coat.

- Mr. and Mrs. Eveland, who were the managers of the opera house in the early 1900s. The UPP team believes that they have communicated with both of their spirits on more than one occasion.
- Frank, a spirit that UPP team members met one time in the catwalk area. They are now trying to gather more information about this spirit.
- An unknown female, who may have been the woman who died of a massive heart attack in the front row of the opera house, just prior to a Statler Brothers concert. They are not sure if it is the spirit of this particular woman and are continuing their investigation.
- The last spirit may not be a ghost, but an entity, something that has never been human. This is the notorious black mass known to dwell in the black hole basement area. The mass was captured on DVR cameras, photographs,

and seen by dozens of people. The entity has told investigators to "get out." In addition, it has hit an investigator on the back of the head and punched a woman in the stomach, causing her to throw up. It has also "gone through" investigators, making them ill. The mass can raise and lower temperature, once lowering it by 19 degrees in a small area of the basement, before raising it to the original temperature of 68 degrees. It has touched both men and women in a personal, uninvited way. "The mass could very well be the entity that we call Charlie, but we're not sure of that yet," said Glosser.

Marty Myers, public relations manager for UPP, believes in the ghosts inhabiting the Twin City Opera House. "I was breaking down a tripod and camera around 3:00 a.m. after an investigation, when I saw a shadow man walk past me on my left about eight feet or so away," said Myers. "I saw the figure very clearly walk about 20 feet before stepping into the shadow of a support column where I lost sight of it."

Myers' upbringing on his grandfathers' Ohio farm was the backdrop for his interest in ghosts and the paranormal. During his formative years, he heard old family ghost stories told around campfires. "My mother was a fine storyteller who grew up near the 'Hornet Spook Light' in Missouri and spent many nights watching the mysterious light winking up and down the dark country road," he said. Myers continued, "I heard tales of ghosts' cars offering hitchhikers rides, phantom footsteps eternally circling old haunted graveyards and spectral ladies floating across roads to be struck by cars late at night." These and other stories created a fertile ground in which his interest in all aspects of the paranormal grew. It wasn't until 2005, however, that he began to take a more serious approach to the subject and began investigating stories of hauntings by himself.

In 2008, he became a member of his first organized paranormal research team, the Central Ohio Ghost Squad (COGS). His first investigation with the team was of the Moonville Tunnel, a place that he had visited many times by himself on independent investigations. He eventually became the Case Manager for COGS, taking over that position around January of 2009 to January of 2011. At this time, he and the other current members of UPP left COGS to establish the United Paranormal Project.

During his investigations of the theatre, first with COGS and then with UPP, Myers became a fan of the Twin City Opera House. "I feel really lucky to have the opportunity to investigate the opera house repeatedly and to have experienced so many different types of paranormal activity there. After all of the investigations at the opera house, I am still eager to get back into the place and see what will happen next," said Myers. He continued "I feel like it is a story still unfolding right before my eyes each time I am there."

Brendan Shay, UPP tech manager, has his own story about an experience with the ghosts of the theatre. "I've had many experiences with the spirits in the opera house," said Shay, "but the most memorable took place on the catwalk. I was on an investigation, when suddenly I felt something pull hard at my pant leg."

Aside from ghosts with and without names popping out to possibly grab someone at every turn in this uber-haunted location, the old opera house also has other secrets. There are a series of tunnels that run under the structure. Stories have been told that the tunnels were used by the "underground railroad" to help slaves escape to freedom. Other stories connect the building that once stood on the opera house foundation to other locations in town and to the banks of the Muskingum River. During the 1930s one of the tunnels was filled in. The townspeople were afraid that the tunnel, which was located beneath the road, would not be able to withstand the weight of increased traffic.

No one today really knows the reason why the tunnels were created. The explanation may be hidden within the dark labyrinth of the underground passageways. Perhaps the answer may never be known.

The Twin City Opera House rarely gives up her secrets.

Ouija: Parlor Game or Doorway to the Unknown

Handmade Ouija Board.

OUIJA, *A Wonderful Talking Board. Interesting and mysterious; surpasses in its results second sight, mind reading, clairvoyance; will give intelligent answer to any question. Proven at patent office before patent was allowed. Price $1.50 – Hollis St. Theatre program, November 7, 1891, Boston Massachusetts*

The Ouija Board, also known as the spirit board, talking board, or more colorfully, the witchboard, is a uniquely American invention. The Ouija is a flat board, made of wood or other materials and usually features the letters of the alphabet and numbers "zero" through "ten," as well as the words, "hello," "goodbye," "yes," and "no," imprinted upon its surface. The talking board has been at the center of a storm of controversy since before it was patented in its modern form in 1891.

A planchette, or heart shaped indicator on coasters, is positioned on the board and one or more individuals place their hands on the device and wait for it to begin to move.

As the planchette begins to wander around the board, it will stop and rest briefly above or on the printed letters, numbers, and words. This is the mechanism through which communication with the dead is said to occur. Whether the results achieved through the use of the board are due to the ideomotor response, the body moving the planchette without the mind's knowing participation, or through the hand of a spirit, many people swear by its authenticity.

The meaning of the word "Ouija" is still shrouded in mystery. "People generally believe that the word 'Ouija' comes from the French and German words for yes: oui and ja. However, no one really knows how the name came into use," said Gene Orlando, the curator for an online wealth of information relating to the Ouija, The Museum of the Talking Boards. He has researched the topic of talking boards extensively. Individuals can visit the site at: www.museumoftalkingboards.com. "One story has it that Charles Kennard, the first manufacturer, called his new board Ouija (pronounced wE-ja) after the Egyptian word for good luck. Ouija is not Egyptian for good luck, but since the board reportedly told him it was during a session, the name stuck," said Orlando

The first patent for the Ouija board was filed on May 28, 1890 and granted on February 10, 1891. Elijah J. Bond was listed as the inventor and his business partners were Charles W. Kennard and William H.A. Maupin. "However the use of alphabet boards with moving indicators goes back to the 1850s. In 1886, there was a talking board craze that took over several states and it was reported in the news coast to coast," said Orlando. He continued, "People held sessions with homemade Ouija boards assembled from available materials, although they weren't called 'Ouija,' of course. Some smart Baltimore capitalists got wind of it, patented the board, and produced it in local factories. The rest is history."

Orlando's massive collection of talking boards is just one area of acquisitions in which he is interested. "I collect oddities, talking boards are a part of my collection," said Orlando. However, his interest in the Ouija as an art form sparked his interest in developing the online museum. "It occurred to me that talking boards, the generic name for Ouija boards, were a lost American art form. Most people knew about the current Parker Brothers Ouija but they had no idea there were hundreds of other different ones all with distinct personalities. I created the site to kick-start an interest in Ouija boards and to bring together others who might also be inspired. It's been quite successful in that regard," said Orlando, who is a regular user of the talking boards. "I do it for my own amazement," he says.

However, he does not think that the Ouija board provides a conduit to the dead. "I don't think I have ever talked to a dead person using the Ouija board. Many of my friends and acquaintances claim they have and that is fine with me. Who am I to argue? It's a very personal thing," said Orlando. He continued, "As far as the successful, positive use of the Ouija board goes, that is well documented. The Ouija board has been inspirational for many writers, poets, artists, playwrights, and a few famous businessmen. Some credit the Ouija for their finest work," said Orlando. Some of the people he may be referring to are: Poet James Merrill, who gave credit to the Ouija in helping him write the poem, "The Changing Light at Sandover;" Writer Sylvia Plath wrote "Dialogue over a Ouija Board" about her experiences from a session with the board. She also wrote a poem about the phenomenon; and writer John G. Fuller wrote a book about the Eastern Airlines Flight 401 crash in 1972 over the Florida Everglades, based in part it is reported, on Ouija board contacts with the spirits of the dead. The pilot and co-pilot, as well as the ghosts of the ten flight attendants who died in the crash kept showing up on another plane, the only other Lockheed L-1011 the company owned and the exact replica of the one in which they died. These individuals, as well as, other artists, writers, politicians, and people in many other lines of employment have claimed that the talking board has influenced their work.

Some of the individuals who have used the board with successful results, eventually denounced its use, such as Poet James Merrill. At the end of his life Merrill dissuaded others from using the board. The band Mars Volta developed an album from their experience with the talking board. But after a miserable run of bad luck, burned the board and then buried it for good measure.

Countless others who are not so well known in their respected fields have had memorable experiences with the Ouija. Martha Workman, of Lewisburg, West Virginia, reported that she had several interesting encounters with the Ouija board as a teenager. When she was 13 years old she received a board as a gift from a friend. She was alone in her bedroom when she had her first experience with the talking board. It gave her a false response to her first question, telling her that her brother would marry a woman named Bonnie. This never occurred.

On another day, while alone in her bedroom again, she was asking the board a series of questions when she took her fingers off of the planchette and it moved by itself. She gathered her courage and asked who was manipulating the indicator. In response, she reports that the planchette flew from beneath her fingers and across the room.

Her next encounter with the Ouija came when she and a friend were sitting side by side with the board on their knees. They were asking a series of benign questions and after taking their fingers off the board, the planchette continued to move and spelled out "I am here." The board then allegedly levitated and flew across the room, hitting the wall before falling to the floor. The two frightened girls then cut the Ouija into pieces with an axe, before burning the remains. Her father, Junior Workman, came by and saw them burning the Ouija board and when they told him what they were doing, he responded, "That might be a good idea."

That was the last time that Workman has ever pursued a relationship with the Ouija.

Orlando has a different opinion of the board's reputation for bad luck and worse. "Well, you have a scary thing here. The Ouija board is pretty much condemned by religious circles across denominations. Talking to the dead is not perceived as wonderful thing to do. They are DEAD, after all," said Orlando. He continued, "Almost as strident are the disbelievers who rail against it as superstitious nonsense. Then you have those who are so frightened by spooks that they can't discuss it without breaking out in a cold sweat. Everyone has an opinion about the Ouija board and this didn't happen over time or little by little. Although created commercially as a parlor game, it's never been benevolent and wild stories and overactive imaginations have just added to the excitement. Not to mention the occasional unhinged individual whose claims that the Ouija made them do it, whatever 'it' was. And that's the whole point. The Ouija board is controversial and it has an attitude. Otherwise, it would just be another forgettable curiosity. So, I have to ask you. What could be more fun than that?"

To those who think that the Ouija board is a dangerous instrument of communication with spirits, or in the worst case scenario, negative entities, Orlando has some advice. "They should never use a talking board. To do otherwise would be to go against everything in which they believe."

"Besides," Orlando said, "the Ouija has a reputation to maintain."

All Hallow's Eve

THE nights are getting longer; there is a chill in the air. This is the time when the veil between the worlds is at its thinnest and the dead are allowed to walk upon the earth. The drapery of night now hides creatures both wonderful and terrifying. This is the time of All Hallow's Eve.

All Hallow's Eve, a celebration of the end of the harvest and beginning of the fallow period of the year, held great importance in Celtic cultures. In their belief system the Celts, a diverse group of tribes in Iron Age and Roman-era Europe, thought that it was the time when the great sun god died. The god would be reborn when the days began to lengthen and the earth once again readied itself for the production of crops. October 31st was the time marking the end of summer and its abundance and the beginning of a cold and bleak winter. The Celts called their celebration of this important event in their culture Samhain (pronounced sow-in). We now call it Halloween.

The word Halloween derives from the Old English era and is a Scottish variation of All Hallow's Even. Samhain is Old Irish and translates roughly to "summer's end." All reference the closure of one year and the birth of another. Samhain, as practiced by the Druidic priestly class of the Celtic peoples, was a fire festival. A central bonfire would be lit and every inhabitant of that area would extinguish the fire in their hearth to be relit by an ember from the sacred fire. This ritual was to bring them health and prosperity during the long brutal winters in a time of undependable heating systems.

The holiday itself was a magical time for the ancient Celts. It was thought that a household could leave offerings of food and drink to appease the spirits that were wandering the earth because of tears in the veil between this world and the next. The "dumb supper" evolved from this practice. The event entails encouraging a deceased loved one to visit the family by placing a plate of food on the table for them. During the entire dinner, no one spoke. This was to further encourage the spirit to join the family on Samhain night.

To frighten away malevolent spirits, people would carve jack-o'-lanterns out of turnips and sometimes potatoes, place an ember inside and set them outside to act as sentinels. The legend behind the practice of jack-o'-lanterns involves the tale of Jack, a villainous Irishman who was both a swindler and heavy drinker. He was able to outwit the devil who then promised Jack that he would never take his soul. After Jack died shortly thereafter, he went to Heaven's gate, only to be turned away for his wicked deeds. He then fled to Hades and was denied entrance there also. Because Jack was now doomed to roam the earth for eternity the devil, in a sarcastic move, gave him a hollowed out turnip with an ember inside to help light his way.

Ancient Celtic citizens, in addition to dodging the denizens of the hereafter on this dark night, were also on guard for the march of Faerie armies. Faeries today are thought of as beautiful creatures with gossamer wings, whose job it is to, well be beautiful. That was not the version of this mythical creature that the Celtic people held. Faeries could be fearsome, warrior-like creatures that could carry an unwary victim off to their world, never to be seen or heard from again.

By the year 800 Pope Boniface IV had designated November 1st as All Saints' Day, the day on which to honor all saints and martyrs. This was done to Christianize the pagan Celtic festival of the dead with an official church holiday. In addition, November 2 was declared All Souls' Day to honor the dead. The three celebrations, each focusing on the concept of death, became known as Hallowmas.

When the potato famine of 1845 – 1852 devastated Ireland, more than a million people died and another million emigrated from the country, earning this event the name *an Gorta Mór*, "the Great Hunger." These refuges brought their traditions, such as the jack-o'-lantern, with them to America. They switched the turnips for publications around the world. A book on the Djinn was a natural progression for the wide ranging topics on which she has written.

Her research into these mystical beings started decades ago. "I have been interested in the Djinn since the 1980s. The deeper I have gone into investigations of hauntings and portals, the more convinced I became that the Djinn are behind much of this activity," said Guiley. She continued, "Yet few people in the West know anything about them. They are not just stuff of legends and fables – they are real entities, and they have a hidden presence in our world."

The Djinn are described as being created before man and are jealous of the new upstarts. However, there is no comparison of the Djinn and fallen Angels in their relationship to God.

"The Djinn are not fallen angels-turned-demons, but they did get cast out for not bowing to Adam," said Guiley. "Some of them act in demonic ways against humans, but they should not be confused with demons. They have their own dimension, their own society. Some of them interact with us and some do not," she said.

The Djinn are noted for their vengeful nature. "Lore establishes that the Djinn are quick to take revenge if they are harmed or wronged," said Guiley. She continued, "Like humans, Djinn are benevolent, neutral, ambivalent, tricky, and malevolent. They come in all stripes. They can be companions, even spouses. There are rituals for summoning them for help, including healing. However, Djinn have their own agendas, and centuries of commentaries about them tell of them being unpredictable and turning the tables on people."

In some cases, Guiley feels that humans need to have at least a healthy respect for these ancient beings. "They have their terrorists, just as we do," she said.

Because she is such a well-respected writer and researcher, this article would be remiss if she did not share with readers some tips on writing and paranormal research. As an author or co-author of well more than 40 books, Guiley finds it difficult to point to a favorite work. "I can't single out any one topic, as I enjoy all of my work, which runs the gamut from light to dark. At present I am deep into interdimensional entity contact experiences of all sorts, and investigations of portals." Her breadth of knowledge about the paranormal is extensive and amongst the dozens of books she has written there are several well received encyclopedias of supernatural knowledge.

She has interviewed many people throughout her impressive career and had never found herself in an uncomfortable situation until working on a book about the vampire underground.

"I have not been threatened, but some people are less stable than others (and therefore unpredictable). In *Vampires Among Us* I describe a couple of vampires who got wound up during our interview. That was back around 1990 when I met them, and today I probably wouldn't blink an eye over it," said Guiley.

In addition to being a successful author, she is an experienced paranormal investigator. She has some advice for amateur ghost hunters and aspiring authors, "Meditate every day. The paranormal is unseen and requires subtle senses to experience and understand it. If you rely just on equipment you will miss 90 percent of the action. Read and study, otherwise you will have no context with which to analyze things," said Guiley. "As for authors, write what you are passionate about, not what you think will sell. Never give up."

Do the Djinn walk among us? As Guiley said meditate, still the mind, and look around. The Djinn could be looking back.

True Tales of Ghostly Encounters

A ghost story appeals to most of us. It's an easy way to have the thrill of the experience without ever having had an actual encounter with a phantom. However, these brushes with the unknown are exactly what paranormal investigators seek out every time they prepare their gear for a hunt. If you want to hear a great ghost story, go to those close to the source.

One of the best places to hear these preternatural tales is at a paranormal themed conference. These gatherings of true believers, which are held all over the country, draw thousands of people interested in the supernatural to hear experts on a number of topics. Another reason many individuals attend these conferences is to network with others who have similar interests.

Several paranormal investigation teams were interviewed at a recent Central Virginia ParaQuest conference. The conference was sponsored by Seven Hills Paranormal Society and Bedford Paranormal. The number of teams attending the conference provided an excellent opportunity to ask some of the paranormal warriors in attendance about their most memorable investigations.

These are their stories.

Seven Hills Paranormal Society.

Seven Hills Paranormal Society, Tara Bryant, founder. Their investigation of the Trans-Allegheny Lunatic Asylum in Weston, West Virginia, left an indelible impression on this team.

The hospital is known to local residents as "Weston State Hospital." This massive hospital for the mentally ill opened its doors in 1864, during the middle of the Victorian era. The mentally ill of this era owed a great deal to Dorothea Dix, a reformer who made an impact while testifying before the Massachusetts legislature in 1844. Before state mental hospitals were made available to the mentally ill known as "lunatics" during this time, they were housed in a number of locations including county jails, and the attics and basements of private homes and public buildings. Through her efforts and those of other reformers, states established institutions to house this vulnerable population. After 130 years of housing tens of thousands of individuals inflicted with various diseases of the mind, the hospital closed its doors in 1994.

When it was built in phases between 1858 and 1881, it was considered an architectural marvel. The building was designed in the Gothic and Tudor Revival styles, in the Kirkbride Plan. This plan was commonly used in the construction of mental hospitals during the Victorian era. Basically, the building was developed with staggered wings, which allowed plenty of sunshine into each area of the hospital. Fresh air was considered necessary for patient recuperation. Although the hospital was originally built for 250 patients, in the 1950s at the height of its operation the building housed over 2,400 of the mentally ill in abysmal conditions. The structure is said to be the second largest cut stone building in the world, second only to the Kremlin.

It was into this rich environment of departed tortured souls, that members of the Seven Hills Paranormal Society entered. The team was in the process of setting up their equipment in the old Civil War era section of the hospital when anomalies began to occur.

The Founder of Seven Hills Paranormal, Tara Bryant, was setting up equipment when suddenly a cord that she was holding "rippled twice and then was jerked out of my hand." Another investigator, Wanda Pickett, was a witness to the event.

When Randy Williams, another member of the team, came around the corner, she was about to tell him about her experience when, "we heard a loud bam, like someone kicking a metal plate. Somebody had kicked the other side of the door, on the other side of the hall. Wanda and Randy both checked the door, which was locked. A large picture of a blueprint of the facility, which was on two hooks had fallen off the wall."

Other investigators also had encounters with the various mad ghostly denizens of this massive and bleak former home of thousands of victims of insanity. Amongst these permanent residents of the hospital is a little girl named Lilly who is known for being a playful ghost. During the investigation Bryant felt the small hand of a child take her own. She is convinced that Lilly placed her small hand in hers.

The team gathered several electronic voice phenomena during the investigation and one interesting photograph. The photograph shows what appears to be an arm reaching up from the floor.

with the living. The investigator asks a question and the Ghost Box scans through the channels. The box will stop on a frequency and a word or two can be heard before the box begins scanning again. The words that the investigator hears from the box often has meaning for them personally, or in relation to the question.

But, is the box a valid tool, or simply a noisy random generator, worthless to those seeking answers to "what comes after death?"Two well respected investigators within the paranormal community believe in the use of the Ghost Box in their quest to communicate with the dead.

Jenny Stewart, the director and founder of the Paranormal Research and Resource Society, based out of Baltimore, Maryland, believes in the power of the Ghost Box to make a connection with the dead. She also hosts a show called *Attached* on the Para X radio network and travels around the country speaking on the dangers of the Ghost Box and spirit attachments.

Stewart has been using the Ghost Box in her paranormal research since 2008. "My now husband David came across a website ran by Mike Coletta, *UFO Geek* and since he is a HAM operator, he was fascinated with the thought of using a radio to communicate with the other side," said Stewart. She continued, "So, he modified our first Ghost Box, which was used at The Witches Castle in Indiana. After the first intelligent response, I was hooked."

Since her first positive experience with the Ghost Box, Stewart went on to conduct hundreds of sessions with the instrument. "During an investigation on Halloween night 2008, we ran three box sessions and heard three different statements over and over. The first was 'get the dogs out,' then 'furnace fire, get out before fire,' and in the third one we actually heard a gunshot and the words, 'break in, killed, gun shot.' We had no idea what any of this meant and at one point I asked, 'Who will be involved in the break in?' The box replied 'Scott,'" said Stewart. She continued, "Scott was someone who had lived at the clients' home prior to us being there and had been removed from the house when it was discovered he was selling drugs. Fifteen days after the investigation, the dog that was in the room died. The veterinarian could not determine the cause of death."

The story continued that on December 5th the homeowner arrived home early from work and noticed that the house was extremely hot inside.She went downstairs to check the furnace. The front cover had blown off and flames were shooting up and out of the heater. In a few minutes, the whole house would have been on fire. The owner had just had an inspection of the furnace completed.

"In late February 2009, Scott, the family friend, was murdered in a home invasion, execution style with a shotgun. The box had also told us that there would be four males and a female involved," said Stewart. The police arrested, charged, and convicted, four males and a female for his murder.

This case was featured on Animal Planet's show, *The Haunted*.

Stewart is not alone in successfully utilizing the Ghost Box during investigations. Stephen Hill is an author, associate investigator for Eastern Paranormal and founder of Piedmont Paranormal Research, based out of Charlotte, North Carolina. "I would like to point out that there is currently no evidence, which is accepted by science as proof positive of an afterlife or what we refer to as the paranormal. That being said, we can never claim proof, only possibility, as to the cause of activity for which we cannot find a rational explanation," said Hill. "I will never tell anyone that their home is haunted, but rather try to find an explanation for the experiences that the homeowners are having," Hill said.

Though not scientifically proven, Hill believes that standard electronic voice phenomena (EVP) or phantom voices captured on an audio device produce the most compelling data that can be collected at this time. "I was asked to investigate a home where the voice of a child could be heard. The lady who lived there thought she was going mad," said Hill. He continued, "I saturated the house with voice recorders, then we locked up the house and vacated the property for a few minutes. When we returned and reviewed the audio on the recorders, one of them had captured the voice of what sounds like a little girl and she was speaking in full sentences," said Hill. He believes that what he captured on the audio device strongly supports the homeowners' claim of a haunting.

An instance of the alleged ghost radio's power in Hill's paranormal investigative research involved a homeowner's claims of phantom voices and an apparition of an old woman appearing in the kitchen of the home. "When I asked who the old woman seen in the kitchen was, I got the very clear name of 'Ann.' When I asked who else was with her, I recorded the names 'Sadie' and 'Cindy.' I called the homeowner the next morning after the investigation and asked her if the three names meant anything to her," said Hill. "She got very silent and then stated that 'Ann' was the name of her grandmother, 'Sadie,' of her great aunt, and that 'Cindy' was her mother's name. All three had grown up in that house," Hill said. He claims to have had no prior knowledge of any of the homeowner's family names.

Hill explains his belief in the legitimacy of the Ghost Box, "I can understand the skeptics' view of the Ghost Box devices, as I was once a skeptic of them myself. But after three years of experimentation with the devices, I have found that the law of percentages sometimes overtakes the possibility of randomness."

Mike St. Clair, the co-founder of Virginia Investigators of Paranormal Education and Research (VIPER) based out of Roanoke, Virginia, disagrees. St. Clair has been investigating the paranormal since 2008, although he has been researching the topic since the 1980s. His background also includes extensive experience in video and audio production. St. Clair is gaining a reputation in the paranormal community for debunking evidence presented as factual by paranormal teams.

"There is so much evidence that is analyzed incorrectly," said St. Clair. He believes that although most of the erroneous evidence presented as factual is due to the lack of experience of some paranormal teams, he cites the lure of the spotlight as another factor. "There are individuals who want to fabricate evidence for popularity and monetary gain," he stated.

His experience with the Ghost Box is extensive. Starting in 2008, he recorded over

200 box sessions at a number of locations. He admits that he got compelling data that some individuals would call paranormal in nature. "But, the reality is that it was more than likely radio interference due to the fact that the box uses radio frequencies," said St. Clair. "I believe that there is zero possibility that this evidence could be validated due to the use of radio frequencies," he said.

St. Clair believes that all evidence is up for scrutiny. "I believe that there is a zero possibility that any evidence will surface that will prove the absolute existence of paranormal phenomena," he said. "Although this is what we (paranormal teams) work hard for every day, the only ones who know the true nature of evidence that cannot be easily debunked are those who present it as fact," said St. Clair.

The debate over the legitimacy of evidence gathered by means of the Ghost Box will persist. Evidence of an existence of an afterlife will continue to be gathered by paranormal teams from across the world. Whether that evidence will withstand the glare of scientific scrutiny, may be another story all together.

Chupacabra, a Contemporary Legend

Photo of possible chupacabra is courtesy of Ken Gerhard.

IN Puerto Rico, March 1995, a farmer found several of his sheep dead. Mysteriously, three puncture wounds were found in the animals' chests and most interestingly, none of them had blood left in their veins. The towns of Orocovis and Morovis seemed to be plagued by some unknown force intent on slaughtering the villagers' livestock. The vampiric killing spree continued and spread to dozens of towns and villages, as well as the countryside. Before it was over, as many as 150 animals on the island were drained of their blood. The official story from the authorities was that the deaths were due to attacks from packs of feral dogs, or exotic animals such as monkeys, or panthers.

Reports of a variety of animals slaughtered by an unknown beast followed quickly in a number of countries such as Mexico, Colombia, Honduras, Nicaragua, Panama,

Peru, Brazil, and the United States. Several reports in Texas began in the summer of 2004, when a Rancher killed a weird looking and hairless canine type creature that had been attacking and killing his livestock. Named the "Elmendorf Beast," a DNA test discovered that the fallen animal was a coyote with sarcoptic mange.

A variety of reports paint an uneven version of the true physical nature of the cryptid, which came to be known as the chupacabra. Some reports described a lizard like creature, there are witnesses who say it looked like an unusual breed of dog, and still others reported that the animal reminded them of a wallaby or dog that stands on its hind legs and moves with a hopping action. There are some who even wondered if the legend of the beast is just a cover up for alien activity in which governments are complicit. There are, however, several common traits that exist between the reports. The creatures tend to be three feet or taller in height and humanoid in shape. Some reports also gave them special abilities like red eyes with the power to paralyze their prey so as to make an easy meal of them, or wings to make personal transportation a breeze.

Someone who has been on the trail of this elusive creature, whose name means "goatsucker," is one of the nation's most notable cryptozoologists, Ken Gerhard. He is a world traveler, having visited twenty-six foreign nations and 43 states. On his quest to find proof positive of cryptids, or "hidden animals," he has camped along the Amazon, hiked the Australian Outback and explored the Galapagos. He has also explored a number of ancient sites from Machu Pichu to Stonehenge. He has shared the results of his findings on a number of television programs such as the History Channel, Travel Channel, A&E, Nat Geo and truTV. As an author he has penned the books, *Big Bird! Modern Sightings of Flying Monsters* and *Monsters of Texas*. In addition, he has completed research for The Centre for Fortean Zoology and The Gulf Coast Bigfoot Research. He also serves as a fellow of the Pangea Institute.

From a very young age, Gerhard knew that he wanted to be involved in fortean research. "I remember watching a newscast about Bigfoot when I was a young boy and I was hooked. From that point on, I read every book I could get my hands on and watched every show about Bigfoot or the Loch Ness Monster that came on television. But, when I actually got a chance to visit Loch Ness at age fifteen, that had a huge impact on me. I can't really say why I became so interested in cryptids. I imagine that everyone finds the subject intriguing, but obviously the vast majority of people don't take the time to become involved in the search. So, I guess I'm just a little bit eccentric," said Gerhard.

His quest for proof of the chupacabra did not come until later in his career. "The chupacabra really didn't come onto the cryptozoology scene until the mid 1990s and those cases were in Puerto Rico at a time when I was busy pursuing a music career. As far as the Texas version, I first heard about it in 2004 when the Elmendorf Beast turned up. I was initially interested in the man beasts like the Yeti and Sasquatch. There was something compelling about the thought of a gigantic, elusive human-like being lurking about," said Gerhard.

As knowledge of the chupacabra began to trickle into mainstream America, he was tapped to do an episode for *MonsterQuest*, a television show that focused on cryptids of all ilk. "I really became intensely involved when I did an episode for the television show. Three years ago, I met with Devin McAnally who found the Elmendorf Beast, as well as Phylis Canion, who preserved the remains of a chupacabra near Cuero, Texas. Both witnesses were very familiar with animals and really felt that something had been drinking the blood of their chickens," said Gerhard. He continued, "I began researching material for my *Monsters of Texas* book and I traveled around the state for a few years, interviewing lots of witnesses, in addition to looking for evidence of these animals. There definitely seemed to be something going on that was very unusual."

The question remains, why did sightings of the elusive animal begin pouring into authorities, creating one of the world's few contemporary cryptid legends? "The great mystery that remains about the Texas chupacabras, relates to why there are so many of them popping up all of a sudden and why their skin is completely hairless. It was recently proven that these animals are mostly coyotes that have been inflicted with a mite called mange,' said Gerhard. "My recent Facebook post referred to the discovery that, in the main areas where these diseased canids were appearing there are also large amounts of sulfur dioxide being pumped into the atmosphere. This has led me to think that there might be a link to pollution and the sorry condition of these poor animals."

But, does the world renowned cryptozoologist believe in the possibility of a canine type beast who sustains itself through blood? "I am impressed by the number of reports that have been logged in the past decades all over the Americas, but the notion of an extraterrestrial, blood sucking creature really seems more related to our fascination with vampires and not really traditional zoology or evolution. The Texas version seemed to be something entirely different all along, though the claims of blood drinking were familiar. I did discover that the chupacabra legends go back much farther in Mexican culture then we ever realized," said Gerhard.

Although Gerhard's hunt for the chupacabra continues, one encounter with the beast stands out. "I had a carcass that someone gave to me about a year ago. It looked like the other Texas chupacabras. It had been found dead on the side of a road. In fact, several people had pulled their cars over to the gawk at its remains," said Gerhard. He continued, "For several days, I had this rotting thing on my patio in an igloo cooler full of ice; quite a memorable experience! I ended up preserving some tissue samples and burying the bones in a friend's garden, since I couldn't find a taxidermist who would touch the thing."

"The significance of the Texas chupacabra saga is that it demonstrates that there are things running around out there in the woods of the state that are not easily explainable." And, just when it was thought safe to go back into the woods he asked, "If animals like these bizarre, wild dogs exist, then why not some other unidentified species?"

When Death was Grand and the Dead Were Puppets

Victorian era graveyard.

ANYONE living in the Victorian era witnessed the rise of Spiritualism, a new way of looking at the world and the other world. A belief system in which it is thought that the dead can and do wish to communicate with the living. These new mediums, or communicators with the dead, opened the door for public understanding about the existence of ghosts and spirits. Their legacy is that we now have the opportunity to seek out the company of ghosts.

This period in history also gave the world a number of other events, such as grinding poverty for the masses and common diseases with no cures. The result was early death for a number of the inhabitants of the cold, dank dwellings in which the average person lived.

As the Victorian Age is most closely linked to Queen Victoria of England, after whom the era is named, this article will focus on the death and burial customs of that area of the world. The following is a very quick tour of this era and how it developed its unique character and obsession with death. Queen Victoria ruled from 1837 to 1901 and during that time there were a number of events that culminated in the death culture of the Victorians.

The Industrial Revolution saw factories opening in towns around the country. These towns drew the desperately poor to them. Many of the poor had been farmers, but because the wealthy wished to buy the cheapest goods, they imported the same products that were being raised by these local workers. In just a very short time, two-thirds of the farmers were out of a job and looking for work, anywhere, doing just about anything, no matter how dangerous. These towns quickly became cities, whose leaders had given not a thought to urban planning or to the common people who lived in them, their needs, even the most basic of water and sewage, were ignored.

The cities thrived and the population exploded. Because there was so much of it, cheap and disposable labor was the order of the day.

Technology and engineering were making great advances. Steam ships and the railways revolutionized travel, which had been regulated to the horse and buggy.

The rise of a middle-class, factory and business owners, making a buck to the detriment of their employees led to a shift in the social structure. Before this age, one was landed gentry, royalty or abjectly poor. There had not been a true middle class. All of a sudden the currency of the day did not include a title, but the almighty buck. This is when the phrase, "Yes, they come from a good family, but penniless," was commonly used. In other words, you could have the title, but money ruled the day.

Since, for the first time, those without the proper background could achieve a modicum of social status, it was important to show it. Middle-class homes of the day were overstuffed with furniture and their children were told they were better than other, poorer children. In short, they treated the poor as they felt they had been treated by the aristocracy.

Personal charity was a rarity; what is now commonly called philanthropy. The people in this era still believed the Queen had been anointed by God to lead the country, simply by the good fortune of her birth to the royal family. So if you had the unfortunate luck to have been born poor, it was your lot in life, pre-ordained by God himself.

So why should the rich care?

In addition to the middle-class feeling quite grand about themselves as individuals, there was that little matter of world domination as a nation. This was during the time when the quote "the sun never sits on the British empire," was accurate. Queen Victoria's reign was marked by relative peace and expansion. During the Victorian age, the nation gained control of one quarter of the world's total land mass and an equal percentage of its people.

"Far as the breeze can bear the billow's foam, Survey our empire and behold our home," cried the Marquis of Westminster, in a fit of national pride.

England was the center of the world. She called the shots, and the English language became the language of commerce, law and government.

However, all of this change led to a nervous populace eager to control aspects of their world. One aspect that was constant in their world was death.

The phantom of Death was a common companion. Rich or poor, all felt the sting of the unwanted emotion of personal loss as the grim reaper took loved ones gently from their arms, or flung them from life into the hereafter.

All may have felt the agony of losing those they loved, but the poor bore the greater burden.

In the Whitechapel District of London in the 1840's, made famous by one Jack-the-Ripper, a laborer or servant could expect 22 years of life, a tradesman 27 years, and the upper class could live to the grand old age of 45, on average. In Liverpool, 26 years was the average for all who lived in the city during the middle of the Victorian era.

In 1899, infant mortality was still rampant, if you lived in the slums a person could expect to lose over half of their children before they reached the age of one. The working class fared better with 274 deaths per 1,000 births, and the upper class fared the best, losing 126 babies out of 1,000. As a baseline, the current mortality rate in the U.S. according to the CIA Factbook is less than 14 (13.83) per 1,000.

People, especially children were dropping like flies. What was the cause of all this death?

The Victorians were still encumbered by archaic medicine. There were no antibiotics, cut yourself and you could die. Have a child and you could die. Have a gum infection? Just die already. And by the way, do it without any anesthetic, as it was not in common use yet; unless you call a good bottle of whiskey anesthetic.

Poverty prevented the masses from acquiring access to even the menial medical attention available. It was cold then too, so the lack of dependable heating systems helped to insure that the dead, both rich and poor, would be stacked like cordwood until ready for the grave.

But, if you had some nice teeth, a rich person could buy them from you for a few pence, maybe enough for a bit of wood for your hearth and food for your stomach. The teeth might be set into some sort of ivory and used as fake choppers for the buyer.

By ignoring the basic needs of the burgeoning population of poor people, city leaders didn't realize that they were doing themselves a similar disservice.

In 1858, London was embroiled in what was affectionately termed "the big stink." This little known and embarrassing bit of history was the result of a corrupt municipal corporation selling drinking water pumped straight from the Thames into which the city's open sewers ran. Of course, along with the water came typhoid and cholera. It is estimated that as many as 53,000 people died because of this lack of social responsibility.

However, a few dead bodies really weren't enough to persuade Parliament to do anything about it. But the stench sure was. The smell was so overpowering that the curtains "of the Commons were soaked in chloride of lime.. ." A bill was rushed through Parliament and became law in 18 days to provide more money to construct a massive new sewer scheme for London. Death was disappointed.

With factories billowing deadly smoke and no EPA standards to be found, the air became as healthy to breathe as the water was to drink.

And let us not forget poverty. Yes, it was mentioned before, but it truly bears repeating.

Because it was a grinding, life-sucking poverty in which its victims were given no relief, had no hope and were ground to emotional dust by the relentless onslaught of hunger, pain, and death.

The children of the poor followed their parents into the death traps of the factories, mines and other unregulated industries.

The experience of one of these children, Patiente Kershaw, is recounted in her own words: "I never went to day-school; I go to Sunday-school but I cannot read or write; I go to pit at five o'clock in the morning and come out at five in the evening; I get my breakfast of porridge and milk first; I take my dinner with me, a cake, and eat it as I go; I do not stop or rest any time; I get nothing else until I get home, and then I have potatoes and meat - not meat every day."

On May 15, 1842, Patiente's testimony to her gruelling existence in the mines, was gathered by Lord Ashley when he conducted an investigation into the conditions of labour in mines. His report led to the mines Act of 1842 that prohibited the employment in the mines of children under thirteen.

All of these factors created human fodder for the burgeoning funeral industry.

The gears of the Victorian "Death Merchant Machine" churned loudly and greedily, revving into high gear upon the death of Prince Albert, husband of the Queen. She demanded that the country mourn and mourn it did, although not to the extent of the Queen herself, who remained in mourning until her death in 1901.

Because the Queen commanded such a high place in society and she had designated black as the fashionable color, and mourning as the latest trend, the rest of English society followed suit. The society of Victorian England was closed, that is to say ranks were tightly closed around issues such as titles and money. If you weren't one of them, you weren't invited to the club and had no way, such as through education, to ever gain access. However, there was an underlying fear even among the ranks of those who were socially accepted of becoming "the other." "The other" was the one who was not like everyone else, who might be too outspoken, or too promiscuous, or too much of a drinker, or partake any of a number of other vices, or who might have too many original ideas. This society would close in on its own and socially cut them off. One person being sent to social Siberia could destroy their entire family's standing in the social hierarchy, as well as, its income.

Excessive mourning had become an established social custom. To ignore it was to do so at your own peril.

Because in some areas over 50% mortality rate existed among children less than one year of age, poor families, as well as the rich would begin saving for their child's funeral as soon as possible, just like parents save for a college education today.

Many parents would bankrupt themselves to give a proper funeral for their loved one. To do less would be to dishonor the person and themselves in Victorian society.

There is a sad photo that exists amongst the paraphernalia of Victorian history. It depicts several young boys, brothers, who do not have shoes on their feet. Yet the family scraped enough money together to have a photograph taken in an attempt to memorialize their young sister who has died. The meaning of what the boys are doing in the photograph, such as pointing to their deceased sister's empty chair is noted by the photographer on the photo. But, there is one that is not mentioned. The mother's hand lies upon her stomach, where she held the baby for nine months before her birth. Victorian prudery would not allow him to mention it in the photo. But the poignancy of its meaning is not lost on most modern observers. No adult male is pictured, are the children without a father, the mother without a husband?

A popular poem of the time summed up the ache that Victorians' felt at the loss of life and echoes all the way into our own time.

> *A light has from our Household gone,*
> *A voice we loved is still;*
> *A place is vacant in our Home*
> *That never can be filled.*

The funeral industry of the time offered a vast number of accouterments for every pocketbook. Some of the most notable included: mutes, whose job it was to symbolically guard the dead. These individuals would stand near the dead, either outside the church or near the door to the home. Many of the mutes had terrible reputations as drunks and rapscallions. Standard bearers were also often employed; these individuals carried poles with a black flag on the end, emulating the standard bearers of royalty. Professional mourners might also be on the payroll. These individuals had the job of wailing, crying, and fainting, which helped in Victorian culture, to demonstrate the depth of sorrow felt for the recently departed. Gifts given to those who attended the funeral, invitations to the funeral itself, and the list went on ...and on.

During this time of grand funerals, undertakers had earned the reputation of preying on the poor. In 1897, an article appeared in a professional journal concerning the "Universal Conspiracy" against their trade: "It would seem that the whole world was leagued against us...Physicians devote all their energies to cheat him out of a funeral: life-saving appliances are invented for the same purpose, and boards of health seem to have no other object but to decrease the mortician's business...The people should be given a fighting chance to die, in the interest of our trade." Whether written tongue-in-cheek or not, the fact that the article was written at all is indicative of the reputation of undertaker's profession at the time.

An example of a method by which the undertaker would market a funeral to a victim was written by Clarence Rook in 1899, "A series of photographs showed me what I could expect for five pounds, and the additional respectability I could attain for an extra two pound ten."

Part of the accouterments of death was fashion. To insure social respectability, women would wear full mourning for a year and one day. This garb consisted of dull black clothing without any ornamentation. This was followed by second mourning, which lasted a period of nine months. Women were allowed to wear minor ornamentation on dresses still made from dull material. The veil, the most recognizable accouterment of Victorian mourning, could be lifted and worn back over the head in public. Half mourning, a period of three to six months during which the woman would ease back into more colorful and ornamented clothing.

The standard mourning time for a widower was two years but it was up to his discretion when to end his widower status. As an added bonus for the men, they could go about their daily lives and continue to work. Typically young, unmarried men stayed in mourning for as long as the women in the household did.

For the death of a child a period of mourning for a year was common.

Because the need for mourning clothes was immediate, these were actually the first off-the-rack clothing items available to people. Poor folks would just dye what few clothes they already had to the required shade of black.

Mourning jewelry often included the addition of hair. The jewelry could be an intricately cast gold piece decorated by the finely woven hair of the dearly departed. The poor would often do something like braid the piece of hair, tying it with a bow and then attaching it to a simple pin. Like the affluent woman who may have originally owned the more lavish piece of mourning jewelry, the poor woman would have worn the pieces to remember the individual whose hair they held.

There was a number of other mourning accouterments, including veils, fans, gloves, jewelry, photographs, and more.

In addition to the mourners, the home would also be decorated in a lively shade of black to denote the depth of proper sorrow that society expected of them.

Doors were draped in black crape to signify that a death had taken place within that house. Neighbors and friends knew to knock gently on these decorated doors. Some families would leave the door slightly ajar so that visitors could quietly enter and leave.

In addition, sending flowers in memory of the deceased was a well-known custom.

What may not be as well known is that the flowers would be delivered to the home, where the body was kept before the funeral. The flowers were then grouped together and made into a temporary shrine to honor the deceased. The flowers also served as a sensory mask to cover the odor of decaying flesh, as embalming was an uncommon practice during that time period.

One common practice during this period was to permanently memorialize the faces of the dead through photography. At one time photos were extremely expensive and beyond the means of many laborers. However, when someone died whom they loved very much, they would often pull together whatever funds they might have available to them for a final portrait of their loved one, either by themselves, or posed with the family, in as natural a position as possible.

What may seem morbid by our modern sensibilities was simply a desperate attempt by the family to grasp a moment where the dead might seem to live again. A moment made permanent through the magic of photography.

There are so many photographs of the dead of this era. However, several stand out, including a portrait of what appears to possibly be twin boys, one alive and one, obviously dead in repose; a man posed with a newspaper to give a more realistic depiction of life; a photo of a young girl with her deceased brother; a lovely young girl surrounded by her dolls. This child had probably played many hours with these beautiful dolls and they had meant a great deal to her.

One of the most disturbing is of a photograph of a girl standing with what appears to be her parents. The photograph of the girl is quite natural everywhere except the her eyes. It was quite common during this time to "paint in" the eyes in order for them to look more natural. The awkward positioning of her hands is also notable. The wooden stand behind her is barely visible.

Photographers of the time who specialized in post-mortem photography would advertise that they could be at the home within an hour after death in order to take the photo.

For the poor who had no rest in life, death offered but a brief respite. Until 1832 no commercial graveyards existed. Instead, the rapidly dying population was wedged into small churchyards around the city, or into vaults, often teeming with the dead and subsequent disease, just below the floorboards of the church and the parishioners it held.

Victorian era graveyard.

An 1839 description of the Enon Chapel interments follows: "This insect, a product of the putrefaction of the bodies, was observed on the following season to be succeeded by another, which had the appearance of a common bug with wings. The children attending the Sunday School held in this chapel, in which these insects were to be seen crawling and flying, in vast numbers, during the summer months, called them 'body bugs.' The stench was frequently intolerable."

This chapel in a physical space of 60 feet by 29 feet and six feet deep interred some 12,000 bodies in a space of 20 years.

James Payne in 1867 wrote in the *Last Homes of the Londoners* : "Thirty years ago, the last home of even a wealthy Londoner was a crowded vault beneath some church hemmed in by houses; while that of the poorer sort could hardly be called a resting-place, since, sooner or later their bones had to make way for the more recently deceased and were thrown to the left and right by the grave-digger. Higher and higher grew the half-human churchyard, shutting out window after window of the many peopled houses round from outlook and air, and substituting for the one a wall of rank rich grass, whose greenness speaks not of life and spring-time, but of death and corruption and for the other, the pestilence that walketh in the noonday and the night alike. Even in the vaults of so-called fashionable churches, not only were no pains taken to render death less abhorrent, but it was positively made more hideous by circumstance. The tawdry pomp of crape and baton, of pawing horses and nodding plumes, and all the hired panoply of sorrow, went no further than the grave's mouth."

How bad was the cemetery overcrowding? St. Martin's churchyard, measuring 295 feet by 379 feet in the course of ten years received 14,000 bodies. St. Marys, in the Region of the Strand, and covering only half an acre in fifty years received 20,000 bodies, A Methodist Church in New Kent Roade beneath the floor of that church measuring 40 yards long, 25 wide, and 20 high, 2,000 bodies were found in wooden coffins, stacked one on top of the other.

Because churches charged the next generation of parishioners for temporary use of the land, they would dig up remains and send them to the Charnel House for disposal. Out with the old and in with the new. Only, according to a grave digger in 1852, some may have been in the ground as little as three weeks. Large pits were left open until they were filled to the brim with coffins before covered with as little as a foot or so of dirt.

Thus was the deplorable state of burial grounds in Victorian England until the arrival of the Magnificent seven in 1832. This allowed the "haves" to further separate themselves from the "have nots."

This time the separation would occur after death. Now, because private companies could provide large, lush garden cemeteries for a price, the dead could, if not take it with them at least surround themselves by symbols of their wealth.

For the first time and for those who could afford it "Rest in Peace," took on a whole new meaning.

But, all good things must come to an end and the death knell for the Victorian era itself began to sound.

tumble neighborhood back in the day. This was a place where card games could cost lives, whiskey flowed freely, and women were available for a price. A maelstrom of emotions, life, and most especially death, occurred in and around the hotel and left an indelible impression on the past that is still experienced by some today.

Although the French founded the city, calling it La Nouvelle-Orléans, and it survived the great hurricane of 1722, the Spanish took control in 1763. The French colony was ceded to the Spanish Empire as part of the Treaty of Fontainebleau.

This transition in leadership of the city came with a heavy price to the Spanish. The new occupants added to the mounting death toll extracted by the harsh environment. Two fires raged through the city during the last third of the Spanish period. In the Great New Orleans Fire of 1788, 856 buildings burnt to the ground on Good Friday. Many lives were lost. A story is told that when the blaze first started people ran in a panic to the church, the Church of St. Louis, and told the priest to sound the alarm. The priest told them as good Catholics they could not sound the bells on such a holy day. The city proceeded to burn to the ground, including the church.

Only six years later, another fire leveled 212 buildings. Again, there was a substantial loss of life. The two fires are the reason that there are only three buildings left in the Vieux Carré of French design. The city was rebuilt in the Spanish style with bricks and firewalls. This is also why there are so many structures in the French Quarter that feature beautiful courtyards.

Although lovely and friendly to visitors, New Orleans is said to be a city that decides who stays and who leaves. If she wants someone to stay within the bosom of her city limits, she makes it possible. If not, she throws them back, like a small fish.

McDowell's story, however, is unique among those of the many other transplants to the Big Easy. "When I was living in Chicago years ago I was ill and was sleeping in the basement of my parent's house where it was cool, when I was woken by a flat tone. I got out of bed and walked to the corner of a bar that was in the room. That was the location of a wall where my baby picture had hung since 1973, when we moved into the house. The photo had been taken down to be put into a new frame, because the old one had broken. As I began to walk past the wall, I turned and looked because the area appeared to be getting darker. I stood there staring and the darkness grew until it looked like a tunnel," said McDowell. He continued, "All of a sudden figures began walking out of the tunnel and I just stood there looking at them. A well-dressed black couple appeared who seemed to be clothed in garments dated from the antebellum period and another man appeared who was clothed in French armament. He had the sword and everything. I reached out to touch the wall and then everything just stopped. The wall was solid again," he said.

"A month ago I was engaged to be married and had a job as a limousine driver. I had a good life and everything was going nice," said McDowell. His life was then turned upside down. "My fiancé and I decided not to get married. I was tired of living in Gary, Indiana. So, I sold my car and jumped on a bus to New Orleans. I had never been here a day in my life and had no family or friends here. I just said 'hey why not.'"

Rodney McDowell in the Historic French Market Inn Courtyard with Patrick, the hotel cat.

Because he only had enough money for two weeks rent, McDowell worried that he wouldn't be able to find a job. He had discovered that most service positions are filled beginning in September, during the tourist season. He then met Nancy, an employee of the Historic French Market Inn, while eating at a local fast food restaurant. Because he was dressed in black pants and a white shirt, the hotel's uniform, she thought he was already employed with her company. When they began talking, she told McDowell about the open bellman's position at the hotel. He applied and got the job.

McDowell is convinced that he was told of his future connection to New Orleans through a vision many years ago. The City did seem to welcome him as part of her

A Brief History of Ghosts

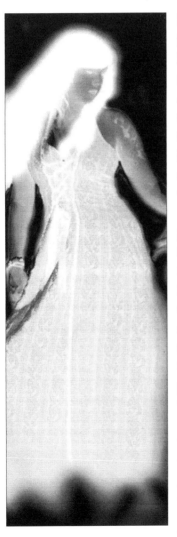

SPIRIT or figment of the imagination, the concept of the ghost has been with mankind for thousands of years. Homer's *Illiad* describes an event in which Patroklos appeared to Achilles (Achilleus) and said, "You sleep, Achilleus; you have forgotten me; but you were not careless of me when I lived, but only in death. Bury me as quickly as may be, let me pass through the gates of Hades..." Hades, in addition to being the name of the God of the netherworld, was the place in Greek mythology where the dead dwelt.

This theme of the return of the spirit to demand proper disposal of their corporeal remains appears in a number of these ancient ghost stories. One well-told tale described several failed assassination attempts on the life of Caligula, emperor of Rome, before he was dispatched by the Praetorian Guard. During his reign as emperor, Caligula had been harsh to the ruling class and many of the nobility and senate members knew about the assassination planned by the Guard. The price he paid for his cruel reign was that no one felt compelled to warn him about his impending death.

Caligula's spirit seemed to have been unhappy with what was done to his body, a quick cremation without the proper pomp and circumstance afforded to other Roman emperors. Individuals reported that he haunted the Lamian Gardens where his ashes were interred. Only after his remains were properly buried did reports of his haunting cease.

Another ancient ghost story describes the return of the wife of Aeneas who was burned during the sacking of Troy. As a phantom, she returned to the earthly realm to console her grieving husband. The return of a spirit to assist the living was a common theme in ancient stories of ghostly activity.

Several early stories of hauntings also used the concept of the ghost as a way to make a moral statement. Cicero, the great Roman author and statesman, wrote of Simonides, a kind and generous soul, who buried the body of a complete stranger. This afforded the individual a degree of respect in death. When Simonides was about to board a ship, which was set to sail, the ghost of the individual whom he had buried came to him and warned him not to board the ship. He took the warning to heart. Simonides found out later that the ship had been lost at sea. The ghost had saved his life.

The first haunted house story may have been written by Roman author and statesman Pliny the younger. He wrote about a villa in Athens that was impossible to rent because of an active ghost. This unwanted resident would terrorize those in the house with the clanking of chains, moaning, and other sundry and disturbing noises. The noise would reach a crescendo at which time an old man would appear, quite disheveled in appearance with a matted beard and hair. The chains were attached to the man and as he dragged them along, pitiful moans escaped the form of the phantom.

Ghosts continued to be a part of folklore in cultures around the world as generations grew old and died and the next generation wondered if the last had been added to the spirit world. The public's interest in ghosts came to a head during the 1840's and the establishment of a new belief system. Those who practice Spiritualism believe in the existence of one God, while also believing that spirits of the dead residing in a spirit world can be contacted through mediums. The Fox sisters, Leah, Margaret, and Kate are given credit for the development of Spiritualism. They appeared on the public stage as individuals who could communicate with the dead. As they toured cities around the country their séances became very popular. Maggie and Kate Fox eventually came forward and renounced their ability to contact and converse with the spirits of the dearly departed. Critics cried "I told you so," while believers felt that Maggie and Kate had given the retraction to spite their older sister, Leah, who had married wealthy and had turned her back on them.

All through the Victorian era (1837-1901) and through the early 1930's, public interest in ghosts was at a fever pitch. The one high-profile cynic during that time who actively became a debunker of mediums was Harry Houdini, born Erik Weisz in 1874. With his background in magic, he was the scourge of those who claimed to be in communication with the dead. He wrote of his exploits in a book titled *A Magician Among the Spirits*.

Along the way he lost the patronage of his good friend, Sir Arthur Conan Doyle, the author and creator of the character "Sherlock Holmes." Doyle's wife claimed to be able to channel spirits through her writing. Houdini asked her to channel his beloved mother, Cecelia. After she did so, he immediately questioned why the writing was not in Hungarian because his mother did not speak English.

Today's ghost hunters also take a scientific and critical look at spectral evidence. Well-known ghost hunters such as Grant Wilson and Jason Hawes of "The Ghost Hunters" have advanced this scientific focus. Paranormal research teams, which can be found in towns and cities across the globe, also make use of scientific equipment and

Time to Celebrate Time

THE incessant ticking of the clock is quieted for just a moment each year as the death of one year gives rise to the next. As the dawn of a new 12 month cycle begins, it brings infinite possibilities; people from all over the world will herald a new phase of time. Many of these same people will mark the eve of December 31, as the date of the biggest party of the year.

The celebration of the New Year can be traced back to the dawn of man. As soon as humans were able to comprehend that there was a cycle of seasons, when one set of seasons stopped and the next began, they honored the event. In ancient Mesopotamia, 2000 years before the birth of Christ, the people noted the return of the fertile earth in mid-March, at the time of the vernal equinox. They viewed the renewed cycle of seasons as a fresh start for the whole world.

The recognition of January 1st on the calendar as the beginning of the new seasonal cycle is a fairly new occurrence on the vast timeline of history. The lunar-based Roman calendar set March 1st as the date of the new year. The original Roman calendar was composed of 10 months. Around 700 B.C., Numa Pontilius, successor to Romulus and the second king of Rome created the months of January and February. In the year 153 B .C., Rome recognized January 1st as the beginning of the calendar year because it was the month that the highest officials in Roman government began their one year service in office. Many citizens within Rome, however, clung to the old ways and still celebrated the New Year on March 1st.

A bit over a hundred years later, Julius Caesar introduced a revolutionary solar-based calendar, known as the Julian calendar. This new and improved way to count days set January 1st as the date of the first day of the year within Rome and her holdings.

In 1582, the Georgian calendar furthered January 1st as the first day of the year. The acceptance of this calendar was split between Catholic and Protestant countries. Catholic countries incorporated the calendar quickly, while Protestant countries took more time. The British did not adopt the calendar until much later, 1752. The American colonies, part of the British Empire at the time, were using mid-March as the marker for the New Year.

Now, of course, America and England alike celebrate the resetting of the year on January 1. But all countries do not.

China celebrates a bright and colorful version of the New Year known as Yuan Tan. This celebration occurs between January 21 and February 20. Families gather for feasting and visiting with one another. In the streets of cities around the country, a procession takes place that includes dancing dragons and lions. The dancers inside these cloth creatures dance and sway, creating the effect of a living animal to the viewers around them.

They cleanse their houses of bad energy and scare evil spirits away by making loud noise. The noise is of course, offensive to these evil entities and the hope is that if the family members make enough noise, the evil spirits will go away and not come back.

The Celtic cultures of old set October 31 as the last day of the year. The festival was known as Samhain. Great magic and mischief was attributed to the fairy realm during this time, when the veil between the worlds was believed to be at its thinnest point.

Many countries do subscribe to the Georgian and Julian calendars and recognize January 1st as the first day of the calendar year.

In Australia, a trip to the beach is often in order. Families will get together for picnics and enjoy the magnificent ocean views together. Like Americans, the Australians wait until midnight on December 31 and engage in happy noise making activities. Singing, whistles, and car horns are just a few instruments of choice.

In Wales, children will get up early and go door to door singing songs. Their reward for this New Year caroling is delicious treats from seasoned cooks and bakers.

The Japanese New Year is called Oshogatsu and is such an important date to them that offices and factories close so that families can be together. They draw from their *and the dynamics of religious belief upon the fragments of vocalization you are capturing. I have a whole collection just on voices that believe that their particular religion lied to them or that God doesn't want them. And it isn't just because they didn't cross over into the light. These entities are taking beliefs they had while they were alive and translating them into the world they now find themselves in!*

Esposito became interested in EVPs from a technical perspective, "I was doing extreme moding and building computers from scratch," he said. When he was maximizing a computer based recording using infrasonic frequencies, he discovered some EVP tests that had been completed by another researcher. "I had to try and replicate some of the tests. Once I captured my first EVPs, I was completely hooked," said Esposito.

For paranormal teams engaged in serious EVP research, he has this advice, "I want to be perfectly clear about one thing and that is that there is no correct process for approaching EVPs. The field is completely exploratory and needs to stay that way. There are many megalomaniacs out there who try and develop false certifications, rules, and end-all-and-be-all tools. It's elusive at best and abusive at worst," he said. He believes that the popularity of the paranormal field has attracted some individuals who try to control the legitimate research that has been done, rather than come up with something new. "There are no rules, experiment," he encourages.

Research into the paranormal realm is advancing as new technology is developed. The proliferation of audio recorders is just one example. Audio captured on handheld is becoming clearer as recorders are improved, as well as the software that "cleans up" the soundtrack.

Esposito does encourage investigators to implement one step as part of their EVP research. "There is one process that I would recommend to every researcher, document all of your work as best you can and make it available to the public, if possible. Seekers looking to build a base of knowledge that one day may be useful to scientists down the road may benefit from your research," he said. His hope is that one day enough convincing audio evidence of life after death will exist that scientists and mainstream audio engineers will accept EVPs as phenomena worthy of exploration by their established professional communities.

Adding to the existing body of knowledge about EVPs is very important to Esposito. It is one of the muses which encouraged his groundbreaking work in the technologically heavy field of EVP research. Because of the seriousness with which he and other researchers approach their work, defined standards will eventually become part of every EVP experiment. "Scientific method and documentation is very important," said Esposito. He continued, "If teams do sloppy work or in a worst case scenario, fake evidence, they are hurting the field as a whole. There is not enough popularity or fame out there to justify undermining research this important," he said.

During his years as a paranormal investigator, he has had a number of encounters with unseen beings. "I have been jumped by an entity or entities on several occasions over the years, which is always pretty wicked. Investigating places of ancestors and family is quite crazy as well," said Esposito.

Then, there was the Sallie House.

Esposito investigated the house on more than a dozen separate investigations. "The insane EVPs, the physical attacks, the phantom smells and phantom furniture; all were recorded by him and his team during their investigations of the site. "Sometimes the house would feel like a long lost home and then it would turn on you like a savage beast," said Esposito. "The house had a personality and it was a schizophrenic one. It was part wild animal and part spoiled child. It is the only place that I have investigated that to this day I daydream about going back, always," he said.

Paranormal researchers are driven to find answers to one of the greatest questions posed to humanity. What happens to us after death? The research is not glamorous. Investigators walk around old buildings, often at their own peril. It's dark, it can be cold, it can be hot, it can be uncomfortable so, why do it at all? According to Esposito, "there are no armchair ghost hunters. I remember many times being so exhausted from listening to EVP files and hitting my head against the wall just trying to stay awake. But the most important reason for doing this for me is the more we find out about them, the more we find out about ourselves. We are only on this plane for a short time, the more we find out about where we are going the better prepared we will be when we get there."

Photo courtesy of Michael Esposito.

hallway. We had to repeat the process about five times, but sure enough, we were able to duplicate the effect. The video piece of evidence had been demystified.

The next few pieces of evidence were picked up by an audio recorder, which had been positioned on a table in the basement. We went downstairs and once again placed the recorder on the table. As we were in the basement we noticed that every sound from the floor above was carried perfectly through the vents and into the basement. Disappointed, we picked up the recorder and went back upstairs. The audio evidence had, unfortunately, been compromised because of the quality and volume of sound coming from the upstairs part of the house.

When I returned to the second floor of the house, Mrs. X was showing a piece of video that she felt backed up her position that the house was haunted. We listened closely to the audio portion of the tape and there was a strange noise, unlike anything we had heard in the house. The video was shot when she was in the basement with her mother. At the time the video was taken they were stoking the fire. Jennifer Woodward, founder of our sister team HAUNT Paranormal, and I went back down into the lowest level of the house and began hunting for anything that could have made the noise, which by the way, sounded a bit like a small girl crying "mommy."

We quickly put this piece of evidence in the "demystified file." When we opened the heavy metal door of the wood burning stove we heard a familiar high pitched noise. We then opened the door at different speeds and were able to perfectly recreate the sound.

When we reported the results of our investigation to Mrs. X, she appeared a bit unhappy. She is convinced that her house is haunted. And if, as reported in Part I of this story, she was physically held down by something unseen, it may well be that there is something that is unwelcomed residing with her in her home.

Because there are three small children in the home, we cannot readily discount her report. It could just be that we were unable to uncover evidence to support her story. But of course, she lived in her house 24/7, we were there about five hours on one given day. The reason I write that she lived in her house, she has now taken her children and has taken up residence in her parents' home.

Will she return to her house? Probably, but the fact that she is so afraid that she doesn't want to walk through the door of her own home is telling.

Would we ever pronounce a home "clear" of a haunting because we were on-site for a few hours and couldn't turn up anything pointing to a connection to the realm of the paranormal? That is an emphatic "NO!" In fact, we often go back to the same location several times to try to confirm reports of a haunting.

Based on very little evidence, my team would also find it as difficult to declare a location to be haunted. A location that is declared haunted can be a very good calling card for a business like a bed and breakfast. There are many individuals, like myself, who prefer to book a "haunted" location with an interesting history, than a cookie-cutter hotel.

A fascinating story is after all, worth much more than a few new bathroom fixtures.

BIBLIOGRAPHY

FOURTEEN GHOSTS (AND COUNTING)

Glosser, E. (2011, May 19). Director, United Paranormal Project. (P. Bussard, Interviewer)

MacDonald and Mabel (Sperry) Birch. (n.d.). Retrieved from The Twin City Opera House: http://operahouseinc.com/2009MAGIC.htm

History of the Twin City Opera House. (n.d.). Retrieved April 20, 2011, from Twin City Opera House Paranormal.com: http://www.greatappalachianspookshow.com/the-haunted-twin-city-opera-house.php

MacDonald Birch. (n.d.). Retrieved from Wikipedia: http://en.wikipedia.org/wiki/MacDonald_Birch

Myers, M. (2011, May 19). Public Relations Manager, United Paranormal Project. (P. Bussard, Interviewer)

Shay, B. (2011, May 20). Tech Manager, United Paranormal Project. (P. Bussard, Interviewer)

*The History of the Opera House Theat*er. (2009). Retrieved from Twin City Opera House: http://operahouseinc.com/2009history.htm

THE LEGEND OF THE WITCH'S BRIDGE

Bussard, S. (2011, June). Source. (P.Bussard, Interviewer)

McCoy, A. (2011, June). Witness. (P. Bussard, Interviewer)

OUIJA: PARLOR GAME OR DOORWAY TO THE UNKNOWN

Guide to the Ouija Board. (n.d.). Retrieved April 30, 2011, from The Ghost Hunting Blog: http://ghosthuntingblog.theauthorityon.com/guide-to-the-ouija-board/

History of the Talking Board. Retrieved from The Museum of Talking Boards: http://www.museumoftalkingboards.com

Orlando, G. (2011, April 27). Curator, Museum of Talking Boards. (P. Bussard, Interviewer)

Online Spirit Communication Tools. (n.d.). Retrieved April 30, 2011, from Ehow.com: http://www.ehow.com/list_7552722_online-spirit-communication-tools.html

Ouija. (n.d.). Retrieved April 30, 2011, from Wikipedia: http://en.wikipedia.org/wiki/Ouija

All Hallow's Eve

Halloween. Retrieved October 13, 2010, from History.com: http://www.history.com/topics/halloween

Halloween. Retrieved October 14, 2010, from Wikipedia: http://en.wikipedia.org/wiki/Halloween

History of Halloween. (n.d.) Retrieved from Halloween Headlines: http://halloween-headlines.com/stuff/history-of-halloween.htm

History of Halloween. (n.d.) Retrieved from Halloween History: http://www.halloweenhistory.org/

History of Halloween. (n.d.) Retrieved from The Holiday Spot: http://www.theholidayspot.com/halloween/history.htm

History of Halloween. (n.d.) Retrieved from Love to Know Paranormal: http://paranormal.lovetoknow.com/History_of_Halloween

History of the Jack O'Lantern. (n.d.) Retrieved October 13, 2010, from History.com: http://www.history.com/topics/jack-olantern-history

Lane, Sarah (2008, October 17). *Halloween.* Retrieved October 13, 2010, from ClassBrain: http://www.classbrain.com/artholiday/publish/printer_493.shtml

The History of Halloween. (n.d.) Retrieved from Infoplease: http://www.infoplease.com/spot/halloween1.html

Williams, Valerie (2010, July 28). *History of Samhain and its Influence on Modern Halloween Customs.* Retrieved October 13, 2010, from Suite101.com: http://www.suite101.com/content/history-of-samhain-and-its-influence-on-modern-halloween-customs-a264402

The Djinn

Djinn Universe. (n.d.). Retrieved March 4, 2011, from Djinn Universe: http://www.djinnuniverse.com/

Dunn, J. (n.d.). *God's Other People.* Retrieved March 4, 2011, from Tour Egypt: http://www.touregypt.net/featurestories/jinn.htm

Genie. (n.d.). Retrieved March 4, 2011, from Monstropedia: http://monstropedia.org/index.php?title-Jinn

Guiley, R. E. (2011, March 2). Author. (P. Bussard, Interviewer)

Hefner, A. G. (n.d.). *Jinn*. Retrieved March 4, 2011, from Encyclopedia Mythica: http://www.pantheon.org/articles/j/jinn.html

Jinn. (n.d.). Retrieved March 4, 2011, from DeliriumsRealm.com: http://www.deliriumsrealm.com/delirium/articleview.asp?Post=174

Jinni. (n.d.). Retrieved March 4, 2011, from Answers.com: http://www.answers.com/topic/Jinn

The Jinn. (n.d.). Retrieved March 4, 2011, from Inter-Islam.org: http://www.inter-islam.org/faith/jinn.html

Wishmaster. (n.d.). Retrieved March 4, 2011, from Imdb.com: http://www.imdb.com/title/tt0120524/quotes

TRUE TALES OF GHOSTLY ENCOUNTERS

About Sweet Briar College . (n.d.). Retrieved from Sweet Briar College: http://www.sbc.edu/about

Bryant, T. (et al.) (2011, April 1). Founder, Seven Hills Paranormal Society. (P. Bussard, Interviewer)

Dickinson, N. (2009, September 24). *Haunted West Virginia: Weston State Hospital Offers More than a Nice Tour*. Retrieved from Examiner.com: http://www.examiner.com/getaways-in-tucson/haunted-west-virginia-weston-state-hospital-offers-more-than-a-nice-tour

Haunted Hospital: The Trans-Allegheny Lunatic Asylum. (n.d.). Retrieved from Haunted Places to Go: http://www.haunted-places-to-go.com/haunted-hospital.html

Industries, T. (n.d.). *Weston State Hospital*. Retrieved from Architecture of the State: http://www.bing.com/images/search?q=weston+state+hospital+west+virginia&view=detail&id=43E3731851B6EE7A4E52401E7CEB72467359F232&first=0&qpvt=weston+state+hospital+west+virginia&FORM=IDFRIR

Lundy, J. (et al.) (2011, April 1). Founder, Roanoke's Investigation of the Paranormal. (P. Bussard, Interviewer)

May, A. (2011, April 1). Founder, Bedford Paranormal. (P. Bussard, Interviewer)

Spangler, S. (et al.) (2011, April 1). Co-founder, Southeast Virginia Paranormal Investigations. (P. Bussard, Interviewer)

St. Clair, M. (et al.) (2011, April 1). Co-founder, Virginia Investigators of Paranormal Education and Research. (P. Bussard, Interviewer)

Sweet Briar College. (n.d.). Retrieved from Wikipedia: http://en.wikipedia.org/wiki/Sweet_Briar_College

Trans-Allegheny Lunatic Asylum. (n.d.). Retrieved from Trans-Allegheny Lunatic Asylum: http://www.trans-alleghenylunaticasylum.com/

Weston State Hospital. (n.d.). Retrieved from Kirkbride Buildings: http://www.kirkbridebuildings.com/buildings/weston/

Weston State Hospital. (n.d.). Retrieved from Asylum Projects: http://www.asylumprojects.org/index.php?title=Weston_State_Hospital

Weston State Hospital. (n.d.). Retrieved from Absolute Astronomy: http://www.absoluteastronomy.com/topics/Weston_State_Hospital

THE GHOST BOX: COMMUNICATING WITH THE DEAD

Ellis, Melissa, M. *EVPs and the Ghost Box* (n.d.). Retrieved from NetPlaces: http://www.netplaces.com/ghost-hunting/is-this-really-the-end/evps-and-the-ghost-box.htm

Engler, Billy. (2010, November 6). Does the Ghost Box work? Retrieved from Examiner.com: http://www.examiner.com/paranormal-in-atlanta/does-the-ghost-box-work-review

Hill. S. (2011, April 12). Ghost Box Expert. (P. Bussard, Interviewer)

St. Clair, M. (2011, April 15). Ghost Box Expert. (P. Bussard, Interviewer)

Stewart, J. (2011, April 19). Ghost Box Expert. (P. Bussard, Interviewer)

Sumption, F. (2007). *The Ghost Box: A Notebook*. Retrieved from Ghost Tech: http://www.ghost-tech.com/adobe/Franks_box_6-19.pdf

Thomas Edison's Telephone to the Afterlife. (2007, March 12). Retrieved from The Human Odyssey: http://thehumanodyssey.typepad.com/the_human_odyssey/2007/03/thomas_edisons_.html

Treadway, Miles, C. *The Dead Can Hear You! Can You Hear Them?* (n.d.) Retrieved from Ghost Hunters of America: http://ghosthuntersofamerica.com/FRANKSBOX.htm

CHUPACABRA, A CONTEMPORARY LEGEND

Chupacabra. (n.d.) Retrieved August 12, 2011, from Mahalo: http://www.mahalo.com/chupacabra/

Chupacabra. (n.d.) Retrieved August 12, 2011 , from Monstropedia: http://www.monstropedia.org/index.php?title=Chupacabra

Chupacabra. (n.d.) Retrieved August 11, 2011, from The Skeptic's Dictionary: http://skepdic.com/chupa.html

Chupacabra. (n.d.) Retrieved August 11, 2011, from Wikipedia: http://en.wikipedia.org/wiki/Chupacabra

Sightings of Chupacabras. Retrieved August 11, 2011, from Monstrous: http://cryptozoo.monstrous.com/sightings_chupacabra.htm

Alirangues, L. M. (n.d.). *Funerary Practices in the Victorian Era*. Retrieved September 10, 2010, from Morbid Outlook: http://www.morbidoutlook.com/nonfiction/articles/2003_04_vicdeath.html

The Art of Mourning: Death & Photography. (1996). Retrieved October 25, 2010, from the museum of mourning photography & memorial practice: http://antviz.tripod.com/mourningphoto/id15.html

Bartlett, D. W. (1852). *Victorian London-Publications-Social Investigation/Journalism-London by Day and Night*. Retrieved September 10, 2010, from Victorian London: http://victorianlondon.org/publications/dayandnight-5.htm

Cremation vs. Burial. (n.d.). Retrieved August 11, 2010, from Cremation vs. burial in Victorian England: http://www.tchevalier.com/fallingangels/bckgrnd/cremation/index.html

Death and Burial in the Victorian Age: Social Darwinism. (2008, July). Retrieved from Victorian Truth: http://victoriantruth.blogspot.com/2008/07/death-and-burial-in-victorian-age.html

Funeral. (n.d.). Retrieved August 11, 2010, from Wikipedia: http:en.wikipedia.org/wiki/Funeral

Greewood, J. (1883). *Victorian London-Publications-Social Investigation/Journalism-Mysteries of Modern London, by One of the Crowd*. Retrieved September 10, 2010, from Victorian London: http://www.victorianlondon.org/publications4/mysteries-10.htm

"The House of Mourning" Victorian Mourning and Funeral Customs in the 1890s. (n.d.). Retrieved October 25, 2010, from Victoriana: http://www.victoriana.com/VictorianPeriod/mourning.htm

How to Mourn Like a Victorian. (n.d.). Retrieved August 11, 2010, from eHow: http://www.ehow.com/how_4556695_mourn-life-victorian.html

Levins, H. (n.d.). *A Lively Look at the History of Death*. Retrieved August 11, 2010, from Historic Camden County: http://historiccamdencounty.com/ccnews43.shtml

Londons 'Great Stink' and Victorian Urban Planning. (n.d.). Retrieved October 26, 2010, from BBC: http://www.bbc.co.uk/history/trail/victorian_britain/social_conditions/victorian_urban_planning_01.shtml

Luckhardt, A. (2010, June 13). *Unusual Behaviors of Victorian Ancestors*. Retrieved August 11, 2010, from suite101: http://www.suite101.com/content/unusual-behaviors-of-our-victorian-ancestors-a248659

A Memento of Life Once Lived: Victorian Death Photography. (2009, September 29). Retrieved August 11, 2010, from College Times: http://collegetimes.us/a-memento-of-life-once-lived-victorian-death-photography/

North America: United States . (n.d.). Retrieved October 28, 2010, from CIA - The World Factbook: https://www.cia.gov/library/publications/the-world-factbook/geos/us.html

Owens, T. L. (2005). *Paying Respects: Death, Commodity Culture, and the Middle Class in Victorian London*. Texas Tech University: Thesis.

Parsons, B. (2006, January). *Cremation in England Part 1: The early years (1874-1885)*. Retrieved October 26, 2010, from International Cemetery, Cremation and Funeral Association: https://www.iccfa.com/reading/2000-2009/cremation-england-part-1-early-years-1874-1885

Payn, J. (1867). *Victorian London-Publications-Humorous-Lights and Shadows of London Life*. Retrieved September 10, 2010, from Victorian London: http://www.victorianlondon.org/publications8/lights-17.htm

Post Mortem - Info and Photos of Victorian Funerals. (2008, January 20). Retrieved October 25, 2010, from Embalmed to the Max: http://embalmedtothemax.blogspot.com/2008/01/post-mortem-info-and-photos-of.html

The Purpose of the Funeral. (n.d.). Retrieved August 11, 2010, from Wyoming Funeral Directors Association: http://www.wyfda.org/basics_5.html

Reynolds, G. W. (n.d.). *The Mysteries of London-The Grave-Digger*. Retrieved September 10, 2010, from Victorian London: www.victorianlondon.org/mysteries/mysteries-106.htm

Rochester's History. (n.d.). Retrieved August 11, 2010, from Glossary of Victorian Cemetery Symbolism: http://www.vintageviews.org/vv-tl/pages/Cem_Symbolism.htm

Rook, C. (1899). *Victorian London-Publications-Social Investigation/Journalism-The Hooligan Nights*. Retrieved September 10, 2010, from Victorian London: http://www.victorianlondon.org/publications7/hooligan-19.htm

Sims, G. R. (1883). *Victorian London-Publications-Social Investigation/Journalism-How the Poor Live*. Retrieved September 10, 2010, from Victorian London: http://www.victorianlondon.org/publications2/howthepoorlive-7.htm

Spiritualism. (n.d.). Retrieved May 5, 2011, from Wikipedia: http://en.wikipedia.org/wiki/Spiritualism

Victorian Era. (n.d.). Retrieved October 27, 2010, from Wikipedia: http://en.wikipedia.org/wiki/Victorian_era

Victorian Funeral Customs and Superstitions. (n.d.). Retrieved August 11, 2010, from Friends of Oak Grove Cemetery: http://friendsofoakgrovecemetery.org/victorian-funeral-customs-fears-and-superstitions/

Victorian Home Memorial Shrines. (2010, April 23). Retrieved October 25, 2010, from A Land of Deepest Shade: http://alandofdeepestshade.blogspot.com/2010/04/victorian-funeral-flower-shrines.html

Victorian London-Death and Dying-character of funerals and undertakers. (n.d.). Retrieved September 10, 2010, from Victorian London: http://www.victorianlondon.org/death/characteroffunerals.htm

Victorian London-Death and Dying-Funerals-Cremation. (n.d.). Retrieved September 10, 2010, from Victorian London: http://www.victorianlondon.org/death/cremation.htm

Victorian London-Death and Dying-Overcrowding. (n.d.). Retrieved September 10, 2010, from Victorian London: http://www.victorianlondon.org/death/burialgrounds.htm

Victorian London-Disease-'Miasma" and smell. (n.d.). Retrieved September 10, 2010, from Victorian London.org: http://www.victorianlondon.org/disease/miasma.htm

Victorian mourning customs. (n.d.). Retrieved September 10, 2010, from essortment: http://www.essortment.com/all/victorianmourni_rlse.htm

Watson, B. (2009, November 1). Save money, die better: Walmart now selling discount coffins, urns online. *Daily Finance.* http://www.dailyfinance.com/2009/11/01/save-money-die-better-walmart-now-selling-discount-coffins-ur/.

Wynter, e. (1865). *Victorian London-Publications-Humorous-Our Socal Bees; or, Pictures of Town & Country Life, and other papers.* Retrieved September 10, 2010, from Victorian London: http://www.victorianlondon.org

A Haunting in the Big Easy

Cox, D. (n.d.). *Need a haunted hotel in New Orleans? Here's your list, part four (pics).* Retrieved June 7, 2011, from Examiner.com: http://www.examiner.com/haunted-places-in-new-orleans/need-a-haunted-hotel-new-orleans-here-s-your-list-part-four-pics

Haunted New Orleans Hotels. (n.d.). Retrieved June 7, 2011, from Haunted New Orleans Tours: http://www.hauntednewolreanstours.com/hauntedhotels/

Haunted New Orleans Hotels. (n.d.). Retrieved July 14, 2011, from Haunted America Tours: http://www.hauntedneworleanstours.com/hauntedhotels/

History of New Orleans. (n.d.). Retrieved July 14, 2011, from Wikipedia: http://en.wikipedia.org/wiki/History_of_New_Orleans

Kilmer, K. (n.d.). *Haunted Hotels in New Orleans Near Ursuline Street.* Retrieved June 7, 2011, from eHow: http://www.ehow.com/list_6125313_haunted-orleans-near-ursuline-street.html

Krane, J. (1998, March 7). *The Octoroon Mistress.* Retrieved June 22, 2011, from Haunted New Orleans Hauntings: http://www.nola.com/haunted/ghosts/?content/octoroon.html

Lanier, G. (n.d.). *The Ten Most Haunted Places in New Orleans Louisiana to See a Real Ghost.* Retrieved June 7, 2011, from Haunted America Tours: http://www.hauntedamericatours.com/ghosthunting/hauntedcities/NewOrleans.php

McDowell, R. (2011, July 5). Witness. (P. Bussard, Interviewer)

Most Haunted New Orleans Hotels. (n.d.). Retrieved July 14, 2011, from travelNOLA: http://hauntedneworleans.travelnola.com/Haunted-New-Orleans-Hotels/

In Pursuit of the God Particle

Anything but the God particle. (n.d.). Retrieved July 6, 2010, from Guardian.co.uk Science Blog: http://www.guardian.co.uk/science/blog/2009/may/29/why-call-it-the-god-particle-higgs-boson-cern-lhc

Higgs boson. (n.d.). Retrieved July 6, 2010, from Wikipedia: http://en.wikipedia.org/wiki/Higgs_boson

Large Hadron Collider. (n.d.). Retrieved July 7, 2010, from Wikipedia: http://en.wikipedia.org/wiki/Large_hadron_collider

Luttermoser. D. Dr. (2010, July 7) Astrophysicist. (P. Bussard, Interviewer)

Miller, D. J. (n.d.). *A quasi-political Explanation of the Higgs Boson; for Mr. Waldegrave, UK Science Minister 1993*. Retrieved July 6, 2010, from George C. Drimitriou: http://gdimitriou.eu/?p=312

Morgan, J. (n.d.). *Race for 'God Particle' heats up*. Retrieved July 6, 2010, from BBC News: http://news.bbc.co.uk./2/hi/science/nature/7893689.stm

Quest for "God Particle" May Require New Atom Smasher. (2010, July 26). Retrieved July 27, 2010, from Fox News: http://www.foxnews.com/scitech/2010/07/26/cern-quest-god-particle-require-new-atom-smasher

Rincon, P. (2010, June 14). *US experiment hints at 'multiple God particles'*. Retrieved July 6, 2010, from BBC: http://www.bbc.co.uk/news/10313875

The Day the World Didn't End. (2008, October). Retrieved July 8, 2010, from NASA: http://www.science.nasa.gov/science-news/science-at-nasa/2008/10oct_lhc/

The God Particle: If the Universe is the Answer, What is the Question? (n.d.). Retrieved July 7, 2010, from Wikipedia: http://en.wikipedia.org/wiki/The_God_Particle

Webb, R. (2009, October 13). *Time-travelling Higgs sabotages the LHC. No, really*. Retrieved from New Scientist: http://www.newscientist.com/blogs/shortsharpscience/2009/10/is-a-time-travelling-higgs-sab.html

Echoes from the Past

Appalachian Caverns. (n.d.). Retrieved July 19, 2010, from Appalachian Caverns: http://www.appacaverns.com/history.htm

Appalachian Caverns. (n.d.). *Cavern Tours*. Self-published.

Hartley, R. (2010, August). Owner, Appalachian Caverns. (P. Bussard, Interviewer)

A Brief History of Ghosts

Broome, Fiona (2010, December 7). *Ghosts in Chains*. Retrieved from Hollow Hill: http://hollowhill.com/dickens-christmas-carol-real-ghosts/

Ghost. Retrieved October 14, 2010 from Wikipedia: http://en.wikipedia.org/wiki/Ghosts_

Keller, Heidi (2003, December 5). *History of Ghosts & Spirits*. Retrieved from http://angelfire. com/moon/darkchamber/monthsub/msu_ghosts.htm

Lyons, Linda. (2005, July 12). *One Third of Americans Believe Dearly May Not Have Departed.* Retrieved from Gallup: http://www.gallup.com/poll/17275/OneThird-Americans-Believe-Dearly-May-Departed.aspx

Most Americans believe in ghosts (2003, February 27). Retrieved from WorldNetDaily: http://www.wnd.com/news/article.asp?ARTICLE_ID=31266

The History of Ghost Photography. (n.d.) Retrieved from Rocky Mountain Paranormal: http://www.rockymountainparanormal.com/photohist.htm

THE FUTURE IS IN THE CARDS

Case, P. F. (n.d.). A Course on Tarot Divination.

Collins, K. H. (2011, January 5). Psychic. (P. Bussard, Interviewer)

Gabby, D. (n.d.). A Tarot History Timeline.

Lionnet, A. (2002). *The Tarot Directory.* Edison, NJ: Chartwell Books, Inc.

Maiden, C. (2011, January 4). Psychic. (P. Bussard, Interviewer)

Ouspensky, P. D. (n.d.). The Symbolism of the Tarot. *Philosophy of Occultism in Pictures and Numbers.*

Thierens, A. E. (1930). General Book of the Tarot.

Waite, A. E. (1912). A French Method of Fortune-Telling Cards. *Manual of Cartomancy and Occult Divination.*

UFO HUNTING WITH MUFON

Credible UFO Quotes by Prominent Individuals. (n.d.). Retrieved from Irishufology: http://www.irishufology.net/forums/index.php?showtopic=9537

General/Mass Sightings. (n.d.). Retrieved from UFO Evidence: http://www.ignaciodarnaude. com/avistamientos_ovnis/Catalogos%20Casos%20OVNI,Rev.UFO%20Evidence.htm

Harvey-Wilson, S. (n.d.). *UFOs, Disinformation and Deception.* Retrieved from http://greyfalcon. us/restored/UFOdeption.htm

Mutual UFO Network. (n.d.). Retrieved from Wikipedia: http://en.wikipedia.org/wiki/Mutual_UFO_Network

Mutual UFO Network. (n.d.). Retrieved from Mutual UFO Network: http://mufon.com

Schneider, C. (2010, September 21), MUFON Field Investigator. (Pat Bussard, Interviewer)

Studying UFOs. (n.d.). Retrieved from Paranormal Study and Investigation Eastern North Carolina: http://psi-nc.org/ufos.html

Unidentified Flying Objects and the Occult. (n.d.). Retrieved from Encylopedia of Occultism and Parapsychology: http://www.encyclopedia.com/topic/UFO.aspx

Werewolf: Companion of the Moon

Felchner, W. J. (2010, February 1). *Lon Chaney Jr. in Universal Pictures' The Wolf Man (1941)*. Retrieved October 7, 2010, from Bukisa: http://www.bukisa.com/articles/238094_lon-chaney-jr-in-universal-pictures-the-wolf-man-1941

Konstantinos. (2010). *Werewolves: The Occult Truth.* Woodbury, MN: Llewellyn Publications.

Werewolf. (n.d.). Retrieved October 7, 2010, from Ask.com: http://www.ask.com/wiki/Werewolf

Werewolves. (n.d.). Retrieved October 7, 2010, from Gothic Press: http://www.gothicpress.freeserve.co.uk/Werewolves.htm

Werewolf fiction. (n.d.). Retrieved October 7, 2010, from Wikipedia: http://en.wikipedia.org/wiki/Werewolf_fiction

Werewolves: The Myths and the Truths Surrounding Werewolf Legend. (n.d.). Retrieved October 7, 2010, from Werewolves: The Myths and the Truths: http://alam25.tripod.com/

Hunting the Elusive Ghost

Harless, A. (2010, November 26). Co-Founder, HAUNT Paranormal. (P. Bussard, Interviewer)

Sensabaugh Culvert. (n.d.). Retrieved from Haunt Masters Club: http://www.hauntmastersclub.com/places/hawkins_co_tn/mount_carmel/sensabaugh_culvert.html

Sensabaugh Tunnel. (2005, April 22). Retrieved from Ghosts and Spirits of Tennessee: http://johnnorrisbrown.com/paranormal-tn/blog/2005/04/sensabaugh-tunnel.html

Train Station. (n.d.). Retrieved from Haunt Masters Club: http://www.hauntmastersclub.com/places/washington_co_va/bristol_va/bristol_train_station.html

Woodward, J. (2010, November 26). Founder, HAUNT Paranormal. (P. Bussard, Interviewer)

The Ultimate Christmas Ghost Story

Anderson, Hans Christian (1846). *The Little Match-Seller*. Retrieved from Gilead.org: http://hca.gilead.org.il/li_match.html

A Christmas Carol. (n.d.) Retrieved December 8, 2010, from Wikipedia: http://en.wikipedia.org/wiki/A_Christmas_Carol

Dickens & Christmas. (n.d.) Retrieved from David Perdue's Charles Dickens: http://www. fidnet.com/~dap1955/dickens/christmas.html

Dickens, Charles. December (1843). *A Christmas Carol.* The Online Literature Library. Retrieved December 8, 2010, from Literature.org: http://www.literature.org/authors/ dickens-charles/christmas-carol/

Evans, Diane (2010, December 8). *The Story Behind 'The Christmas Carol' by Charles Dickens.* Retrieved from suite101: http://www.suite101.com/content/the-story-behind-the-christmas-carol-by-charles-dickens-a318003

Felisilda, Pascasio JR. *Book Review – A Christmas Carol by Charles Dickens.* (n.d.) Retrieved from ezine@rticles: http://ezinearticles.com/?Book-Review---A-Christmas-Carol-by-Charles-Dickens&id=5518190

Lombardi, Esther. *A Christmas Carol Quotes.* (n.d.) Retrieved December 8, 2010, from About. com: http://classiclit.about.com/od/christmascarola/a/aa_christmas.htm

The Little Match Girl. (n.d.) Retrieved December 9, 2010, from Wikipedia: http://en.wikipedia. org/wiki/The_Little_Match_Girl

VAMPIRE AS LOVER/DRACULA

Belanger, Ed. (2007). *Vampires in Their Own Words.* Minnesota: Llewellyn Worldwide, Ltd.

Dracula. (n.d.). Retrieved July 16, 2010, from Wikipedia: http://enwikipedia.org/wiki/Dracula

Dracula - Beyond the Legend. (n.d.). Retrieved July 16, 2010, from Romania Tourism.com: http://www.romaniatourism.com/dracula-legend.html

Dracula - Myth and Real History. (n.d.). Retrieved July 16, 2010, from Vlad Dracula-The Truth: http://dracula-transylvania.blogspot.com/

Jenkins, M. C. (2010). *Vampire Forensics: Uncovering the Origins of an Enduring Legend.* Washington, D.C.: National Geographic Society.

John Polidori & the Vampyre Bryron. (n.d.). Retrieved July 16, 2010, from http://www.angelfire. com/jazz/louxsie/polidori.html

John William Polidori. (n.d.). Retrieved July 16, 2010, from Wikipedia: http://en.wikipedia. org/wiki/John_Polidori

Polidori, J. W. (1819). *The Vampyre: A Tale.* London: The New Monthly Magazine and Universal Register.

Transylvania. (n.d.). Retrieved July 16, 2010, from Wikipedia: http://enwikipedia.org/wiki/ Transylavania

Trow, M. J. (2010). *A Brief History of Vampires.* London: Running Press.

Vlad III Dracula and his external policy. (n.d.) Retrieved September 24, 2010, from Exploring

Romania: http://www.exploringromania.com/vlad-iii.html

ZODIAC PANIC

A Breeze from the Stars. (2004, December 17). Retrieved from NASA Science: http://science. nasa.gov/science-news/science-at-nasa/2004/17dec_heliumstream/

Braiker, B. (2011, January 13). *So, Now What's Your Sign?* Retrieved from ABC News: http://abcnews.go.com/Entertainment/astrology-controversy-zodiac-sign-wrong/ story?id=12609264

McKinley, J. (2011, January 14). *Did Your Horoscope Predict This?* Retrieved from The New York Times:http://www.nytimes.com/2011/01/15/us/15zodiac.html?_r=1&scp=1&sq=zodiac%20 panic&st=cse

Reiher, A. (2011, January 13). *New Zodiac sign Ophiuchus doesn't mean much for horoscope followers or astrologers - don't panic!* Retrieved from Zap2it: http://blog.zap2it.com/ pop2it/2011/01/new-zodiac-sign-ophiuchus-doesnt-mean-much-for-horoscope-followers-or-astrologers---dont-panic.html

Shapiro, D. L. (n.d.). *Constellations in the zodiac.* Retrieved from NASA: http://spaceplace. nasa.gov/starfinder3/

What's Your Sign? (n.d.). Retrieved from NASA: http://spaceplace.nasa.gov/starfinder2/

Zeitvogel, K. (2011, January 15). *Report triggers Zodiac panic.* Retrieved from News24: http:// www.news24.com/SciTech/News/Report-triggers-zodiac-panic-20110115

Zodiac Panic! Who's Ophiuchus. (2011, January 15). Retrieved from Freaky Phenomena: http:// freakyphenomena.com/news/zodiac-panic-whos-ophiuchus

HIGHGATE CEMETERY: A MODERN VAMPIRE STORY

Beyond the Highgate Vampire: An Interview with David Farrant. (n.d.). Retrieved July 23, 2010, from davidfarrant.org: http://davidfarrant.org/writtenword/interviews/ivm18. html

Encounters with the Highgate Vampire. (n.d.). Retrieved August 8, 2010, from Vampire Research Society: http://vampireresearchsociety.blogspot.com/2009/02/encounters-with-highgate-vampire.html

Farrant, D. (2010, August, 12). Witness. (P. Bussard, Interviewer)

Farrant, D. (n.d.). *The Black History of Highgate: Has the Stone Cast its Magic Spell.* Retrieved July 23, 2010, from davidfarrant.org: http://www.davidfarrant.org/writtenword/articles/ blackhistory.html

Gough, A. (n.d.). *17 Questions: David Farrant.* Retrieved July 27, 2010, from Andrew Gough: http://www.andrewgough.co.uk/17q_farrant.html

Highgate Vampire. (n.d.). Retrieved July 23, 2010, from Wikipedia: http://en.wikipedia.org/ wiki/Highgate_Vampire

Interview with the Real Vampire Hunter. (n.d.). Retrieved July 23, 2010, from davidfarrant.org: http://www.davidfarrant.org/writtenword/interviews/biteme.html

THE MOTHMAN

(n.d.). Retrieved from Mothmen.US: http://www.mothmen.us/silver-bridge.htm

Mothman? (2009, April 15). Retrieved from L.A. Marzulli's Blog: http://lamarzulli.wordpress.com/2009/04/15/mothman/

Mothman. (n.d.). Retrieved from Unkown Explorers: http://www.unknownexplorers.com/mothman.php

Mothman. (n.d.). Retrieved from Wikipedia: http://en.wikipedia.org/wiki/Mothman

Mothman: The Enigma of Point Pleasant. (n.d.). Retrieved from Unexplained America: http://www.prairieghosts.com/moth.html

Pt. Pleasant Span Collapses. (n.d.). Retrieved from Silver Bridge Collapse: The Long Day: http://www.freewebs.com/silverbridgeaccident/newspaperarticles.htm

Walmsley, J. (2011, August). Author. (P. Bussard, Interviewer)

Walsh, D. (2002, January 21). *the mothman cometh.* Retrieved from disinformation: http://old.disinfo.com/archive/pages/dossier/id270/pg1/index.html

A TIME TO CELEBRATE TIME

A History of the New Year. (n.d.). Retrieved December 22, 2010, from Infoplease.com: http://infoplease.com/spot/newyearhistory.html

New Year Celebrations Around the World. (n.d.). Retrieved from Scholastic: http://www2.scholastic.com/browse/article.jsp?id=3750336

New Year Traditions. (n.d.). Retrieved from FatherTime's.Net: http://www.fathertimes.net/traditions.htm

New Year's Eve. (n.d.). Retrieved from Wikipedia: http://en.wikipedia.org/wiki/New_Year%27s_Eve

Silver, T. (2010, December 10). *New Year's Traditions and Celebrations Around the World.* Retrieved from suite101: http://terisilver.suite101.com/new-years-traditions-and-celebrations-around-the-world-a319013

WATER WITCH

Dowsing. (n.d.). Retrieved June 16, 2011, from Answers.com: http://www.answers.com/topic/dowsing-1

Dowsing. (n.d.). Retrieved June 16, 2011, from Crystalinks.com: http://crystalinks.com/dowsing.html

Dowsing. (n.d.). Retrieved June 16, 2011, from Wikipedia: http://en.wikipedia.org/wiki/Dowsing

Dowsing: Subconscious and the Paranormal. (n.d.). Retrieved June 16, 2011, from About.com: http://paranormal.about.com/od/dowsing/a/aa110705.htm

Dowsing: The good, the bad, and the muddled. (n.d.). Retrieved June 16, 2011, from Indiogroup.com: http://www.indigogroup.co.uk/edge/dowsing.htm

The Joy of Dowsing. (n.d.). Retrieved June 16, 2011, from The Llewellyn Journal: http://www.llewellyn.com/journal/article/469

Hospital of Souls

Department of Health (2000, October 5). *Hospital Service License Fee.* State of Tennesee.

Flessner, D. (2005, July 30). *Nashville-based hospital chain will buy Jasper, Tenn., medical center.* Retrieved October 5, 2009, from Chattanooga Times Free Press: http://www.accessmylibrary.com

Flessner, D. (2005, December 2). *New owners of Marion County, Tenn., hospital seek to add physcians.* Retrieved October 6, 2009, from Chattanooga Times/Free Press: http://www.accessmylibrary.com/article-1G1-139325348/new-owners-marion-county.html

Department of the Inspector General (2000). *Hospital Closure: 1998.* June Gibbs Brown, Inspector General.

Henderson, V. (1995, November 14). *South Pittsburg Suit Seeks Info on Fate of Hospital.* Retrieved October 5, 2009, from Chattanooga Times Free Press: https://iis.timesfreepress.com/archive

Golden, T (July 2011). Paranormal Investigator (P. Bussard, Interview)

Jasper, Tennessee. (n.d.). Retrieved October 5, 2009, from Wikipedia: http://en.wikipedia.org/wiki/Jasper,_Tennessee

Lambert, D. (n.d.). *The Birth of South Pittsburg, Tennessee.* Retrieved October 5, 2009, from South Pittsburg Historic Preservation Society: http://www.historicsouthpittsburgtn.org/SPHistory1.html

Lydick, C (July 2011). Director South Pittsburg Hospital. (P. Bussard, Interview)

Old South Pittsburg Hospital. (n.d.). Retrieved October 5, 2009, from LoopNet Property Listing: http://www.loopnet.com/property/15257588/1100-Holly-Ave/

Owner of Chattanooga. Tenn., Hospitals Announces Name Change. (n.d.). Retrieved October 6, 2009, from High Beam Research: http://www.accessmylibrary.com/coms2/summary_0286-5727175_ITM

Sherrill, C. (1995, September 14). *Hospital Location Debated.* Retrieved October 5, 2009, from Chattanooga Times Free Press: https://iis.timesfreepress.com/archive

Sherrill, C. (1998, September 29). *New Jasper Hospital to Serve Sequatchie Valley.* Retrieved October 5, 2009, from Chattanooga Times Free Press: https://iis.timesfreepress.com/archive

South Pittsburg, Tennessee. (n.d.). Retrieved October 5, 2009, from City-Data.com: http://www.city-data.com/city/South-Pittsburg-Tennessee.html

South Pittsburg, Tennessee. (n.d.). Retrieved October 5, 2009, from Wikipedia: http://en.wikipedia.org/wiki/South_Pittsburg,_Tennessee

LISTENING TO THE DEAD

All About Electronic Voice Phenomena. (n.d.). Retrieved August 23, 2011, from About.com: http://paranormal.about.com/od/ghostaudiovideo/a/All-About-EVP.htm

Electronic Voice Phenomenon. (n.d.). Retrieved August 23, 2011, from Wikipedia: http://en.wikipedia.org/wiki/Electronic_voice_phenomena

Esposito, M. (2011, August 5). Electronic Voice Phenomena Expert. (P. Bussard, Interviewer)

EVP: Voices of the Dead. (n.d.). Retrieved August 23, 2011, from Squidoo: http://en.wikipedia.org/wiki/Electronic_voice_phenomena

Experimenting with Electronic Voice Phenomena. (n.d.). Retrieved August 23, 2011, from American Ghost Society: http://prairieghosts.com/voice.html

Strickland, N. (2011, August 4). *An Introduction to Electronic Voice Phenomena.* Retrieved August 23, 2011, from Our Experiences with the Spectral World: http://sdprsblog.wordpress.com/2011/08/04/an-introduction-to-electronic-voice-phenomena